5 NATURAL LAWS

TO

KNOCK OUT

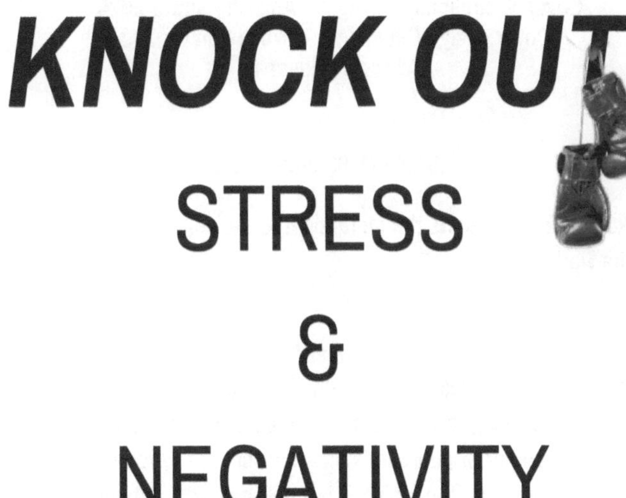

STRESS

&

NEGATIVITY

ANKUSH KANWAR

MATTER BOOK WORLD

An Imprint of Matter Products and Engineering

MATTER BOOK WORLD

"We are tuning our minds to discriminate between good and bad
and
find a way to eliminate the bad
and
how to hold on to the good."

CONTENT

<u>PREFACE</u>

Stress and negativity are the most formidable adversaries of our time, particularly in the information age. Its negative impact on human life expectancy, mental well-being, peace, time, finances, and many other valuable aspects of life cannot be underestimated. We fondly recall the days when making new friends came naturally, and our smiles were ever-present. Our warm receptions for relatives, cousins, and old friends, as well as the exuberant celebrations of family events, are cherished memories. However, the increasing prevalence of technology has led to a shift in these traditions.

We find ourselves less engaged in face-to-face interactions, quieter in social settings, and less focused during work meetings. Throughout the day, we experience various mood swings. Living our lives under the constant pressures of everyday distractions, tensions, *demands, compliances, burdens, and politics, it's easy to lose sight of the vibrant colors that make life beautiful. Viewing our realities through monochromatic lenses, we create an illusion of a colorless existence. The relentless push to excel has become our new normal, leaving us with a stark impression that there is no sunshine in our lives.*

We are seeking solace in our ever-present companions, smart devices, and technological advancements which are at one's fingertips. While these gadgets possess remarkable problem-solving capabilities, why do we continue to grapple with the invisible adversaries of Stress and Negativity? Despite the widespread reach of smart devices and technological advancements, why is the life expectancy of working-age individuals declining? Why do human beings are less satisfied with accomplishments? Why are we constantly yearning for more? Despite the convenience, I can't help but question why we've confined ourselves only to sending online gifts, ordering food online, and connecting digitally with our loved ones during significant life events.

It's undeniable that smart devices and technological advancements have transformed our lives, offering smart gadgets and improved machines of the future.

However, these changes have also brought new challenges, including an increased sense of unfulfillment. As we navigate this evolving landscape, it's crucial to consider whether these advancements truly contribute to our well-being and happiness. Although technology and machines should have improved human quality of life, we are confronted with new-age challenges of sorrow, apprehension, and pessimism. I do not oppose the use of technology, but I urge us to consider whether we can truly address our challenges, problems, and tensions solely through these smart devices.

The joy on a child's face, when you share a joke, is a reminder of the carefree happiness we often overlook in our own lives. We must reflect on our real needs and goals, and make choices that align with them amidst the distractions and complexities of modern life. Living with the same amenities of life some people live joyfully, while others are burdened by stress and negativity. It's time to rediscover the simple pleasures of life: laughing with family, spending quality time with friends, and approaching challenges with confidence. This book will introduce 5 natural laws that can help us conquer the demons of stress and negativity and regain happiness, peace, and self-confidence, even in challenging and burdensome times.

ABOUT BOOK

Imagine a natural stream of water crossing our garden or farm and destroying our plantation. To save our plantation and garden we decided to change the natural water stream flow to another direction along with that we also want to keep a small amount of stream water for the use of our garden. How will we do it? We could start by evaluating the current stream flow and finding a new route for the water. Next, we might consider building barriers or digging channels to divert the stream away from our garden while maintaining access to controlled water for our garden's use. It's crucial to manage the redirection carefully to minimize any potential environmental impact.

Consider the analogy of our brain functioning like a flowing stream. Countless thoughts rush through our minds every second, but not all bring positivity, peace, and happiness in our lives.

Is it possible to channel positive thoughts while diverting negative ones away? We cannot simply block or channel thoughts like we would redirect water flow in a garden. Our thoughts are intangible, invisible entities that influence our well-being. If we could physically manifest our positive thoughts and rid ourselves of negative ones, we would all opt for such a solution. However, since this is not feasible, we must actively seek out and cultivate positive thoughts amidst the countless others that constantly flood our minds. However, there must be a way to achieve this, as evidenced by the success of positive individuals and the struggles of negative or confused ones.

The ancient story of the race between Ganesha and Kartikeya is truly captivating, showcasing the triumph of mindfulness and positivity. In a legendary race, Ganesha and Kartikeya, the divine sons of Lord Shiva and Devi Parvati, took on the challenge to circumnavigate the entire world three times. The victor would be the one who completed this feat in the shortest time. Kartikeya swiftly mounted his peacock and dashed off, determined to achieve his goal. Meanwhile, Ganesha, displaying his positive mindset, chose to encircle his revered parents,

Lord Shiva and Devi Parvati, three times. Ganesha's deliberate actions and the symbolism of encircling his parents as his universe convey powerful messages about the impact of positivity and powerful decisions. This timeless tale serves as a compelling reminder of the strength and power of positivity and the significance of the right decisions at the right time.

There are invisible natural connections inside us, linking our body and mind and influencing each other, we can harness these connections to make impactful decisions and actions in our daily lives. By tapping into these interconnected strings, we have the potential to unearth our true internal powers, propelling us toward success and helping us overcome challenges. In times of sickness, our physical strength diminishes, and our mental acuity wanes. This demonstrates the interconnectedness of our body and mind, emphasizing that they are not separate entities but rather deeply intertwined. Stress and excessive mental work can have an impact on our physical appearance and overall health. Many people experience changes in their physical appearance during intense periods of stress and excessive mental work. It's important to maintain a balance between our mental and physical activities to ensure our overall well-being. Understanding and leveraging these invisible connections, which hold immense universal powers, can lead to a life that is abundant in all aspects.

5 natural laws with a simple step-by-step approach can provide the motivation, energy, and guidance necessary to achieve success and attain the highest levels in our lives. These laws have the transformative power to turn our negativity and weaknesses into positivity and strength, ultimately leading us to a life filled with freedom, success, and comfort. This book is structured with engaging and uncomplicated chapters, allowing you to seamlessly read and apply the content from beginning to end. Upon completing the book, we will gain a new perspective on the designs, techniques, and functioning of our inner world, empowering us to take control of our lives in a better way.

Before delving into the 5 natural laws, it's crucial to understand that our universe, galaxy, solar system, and Earth adhere to systematic designs and laws, this book is also based on natural laws and rules essential for human welfare. These natural laws and rules are inherent within each one of us, such as the power of study, which is accessible to all but most beneficial to those who put in *the effort to learn, grow, and succeed. Similarly, these 5 natural laws and techniques are deeply rooted within us, and only a few have truly capitalized on them. This book will illuminate the path to help us effectively learn, understand, and combat our internal adversaries to knock out Stress and Negativity forever from our lives.*

MASTERING BOXING TECHNIQUES AND 5 NATURAL LAWS

Boxing includes blocking, punches, footwork, hooks, uppercuts, and various other defensive and offensive techniques. To be victorious against our opponent requires our skill, strategy, physical strength, and mental toughness. Mastering these techniques and skills requires 100% dedication, practice, and guidance from our teacher or coach. But after we enter the boxing ring, we are on by ourselves. The time we spent learning techniques and enduring rigorous practices and efforts to sharpen ourselves has led us to this moment to shine and show the world what we're made of. In the boxing ring, we fight and face our challenger's punches all alone, no one from the outside world can help us win. It doesn't matter how talented our coach may be, but inside the boxing ring, we had to prove our worth to the world. Our teacher or coach cannot come inside the boxing ring to help us to defeat our opponent. Similarly, in our internal battles with stress and negativity, we must fight solo to claim victory. Let's overcome these obstacles to live a rewarding and grand life and take control of our destiny.

Our internal struggle holds us back and instills a fear of failure, convincing us that we are unworthy and incapable of achieving our goals. The seeds of negative thoughts draw strength from deep within us and grow into a dense and formidable tree, bearing branches of frustration, sadness, depression, and doubt. These negative emotions cast a shadow over our lives, leaving us uncertain, sad, unfulfillment, and less capable of making courageous decisions. Every natural law serves as a tool to uproot the tree of stress and negativity that has taken root within us. This journey will guide us in cutting away this burden, clearing the path to a life filled with positivity and brightness. Through practicing these 5 laws, we will uncover inner confidence, courage, and life values, empowering us to embark on a journey toward success, harmony, and realization.

Embracing these 5 natural laws will lead us to discover the boundless positivity, joy, and lasting tranquillity within our soul. Understanding and integrating these laws into our daily lives will empower us to harness the forces of nature through our souls, enabling us to accomplish anything and ascend to the pinnacle of success. These 5 natural laws will lead us through a systematic journey, enabling us to comprehend and combat the invisible adversaries that inhabit us, ultimately empowering us to confront the complexities of the external world. By uprooting these adversaries, we can restore bliss, alleviate anxiety, and naturally attain inner peace. As a result, we will experience positive changes in our decision-making, daily activities, overall environment, and social and professional circles. These rules will prompt us to take action, and we will immediately notice their positive impact once we start applying them.

To effectively implement these 5 natural laws to reduce stress and negativity, we need to take charge of our well-being. No one else can cleanse our internal system for us. It is akin to someone buying or cooking vegetables for us but not being able to eat them for us. Similarly, others can provide us with resources and support, but ultimately, we are the ones who must take action. These 5 natural laws are meant for personal application, not just for reading or discussion. By following and implementing these laws, we will become more engaged and empowered to take control of our lives.

CHAPTER 1
<u>FIRST NATURAL LAW</u>
<u>CHARACTER BUILDING</u>

Embarking on our transformative journey, we aim to tap into the profound strength of our soul by mastering essential principles and honing skills through the practice of 5 natural laws in our daily lives. The initial step on this journey involves cultivating a resilient character. In this opening chapter, we will explore the significance of character development. Why does prioritizing character-building take precedence over other chapters, and why is it crucial to commence the journey with this focus? These are important questions and must be addressed before going further and deeper.

Let's draw a parallel to house construction. When building a house, the first step is to create a strong foundation. This foundation ensures that the entire structure can withstand extreme wind, snow, rain, seismic activities, and other natural occurrences for many years to come. Similarly, in learning the 5 natural laws to overcome Stress and Negativity, character building serves as the foundational step.

Character building lays a sturdy foundation for mastering and internalizing techniques in a sustainable manner benefiting us in all subsequent chapters of this book to learn and develop our skills and strategies. By fortifying our character, we equip ourselves to combat external pressures, negative emotions, and old habits that may attempt to regain control all over again in later stages.

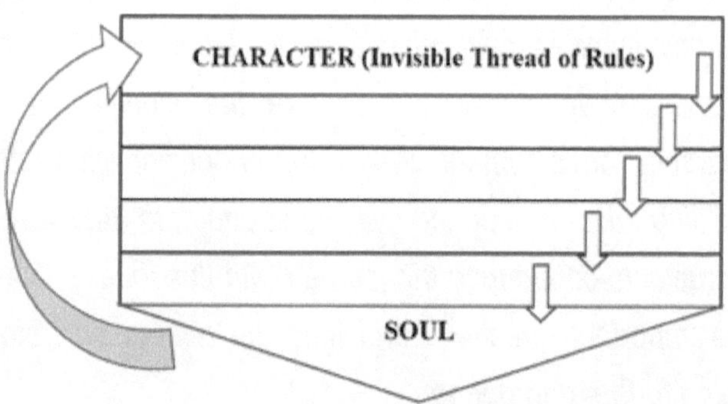

In our society, each person carries with them a defining character that shapes their daily actions and reactions. Our character guides us in decision-making, helping us navigate life's challenges and make choices aligned with our core values and laws. A strong character empowers

us to distinguish between right and wrong and to tackle complex problems with confidence. Our character is a reflection of our core values and beliefs which are shaped by our life experiences, events, and the teachings of our parents, siblings, and the society in which we are raised. In our society, it's common for children to follow in their parent's footsteps, whether it's pursuing a career in medicine, engineering, business, or the military. Many individuals tend to stick to the paths set and suggested by their families and communities for them.

Often, we do not actively work to align our character with our life goals and ambitions. Instead, our character tends to be a product of our environment and the society in which we live. However, some rare individuals break free from these expectations and pursue their dreams by building character in line with their aspirations, aims, and goals. These individuals often stand out and achieve remarkable success by staying true to their unique values, beliefs, and character. We can all think of examples of such individuals who have defied societal norms and carved their own paths to success by building a strong character in our society.The founding fathers of the US, Benjamin Franklin, Marie Curie, Abraham Lincoln, Mother Teresa, APJ Abdul Kalam, and many others who are known as great outfaced societal norms and they went on to become influential figures due to their unwavering ethics, laws, and moral values.

All successful individuals share a common trait: unwavering character. They don't wait for guidance or approval, instead facing challenges head-on to achieve greatness. Success demands unwavering focus, determination, and adherence to personal principles. Our commitment, honesty, and defined objectives are crucial to attaining our aspirations. Building a resilient character enables us to withstand stress and negativity, creating a reservoir of positivity. Though this may initially seem intricate, once mastered, it becomes a potent tool for conquering any obstacle and realizing our dreams.

Developing a strong character is essential for all individuals, be it teenagers, actors, musicians, politicians, business owners, athletes, retirees, or across all walks of life. In today's information-driven world, where technology dominates, it's easy to lose sight of fundamental issues and succumb to the negative impact of stress and negativity. We must prioritize character development and well-being amidst the overwhelming influence of modern technology and information overload. In many cases, we may not realize that we are experiencing phases of stress and negativity. In our fast-paced world, we are often so preoccupied with our daily routines that we tend to overlook our inner turmoil. While we may present a composed exterior, the internal burden of stress and negativity can leave us feeling hollow. To overcome this and alleviate feelings of loneliness, anxiety, sadness, and frustration, we require a natural force that can permeate our being and infuse our hearts and souls with mindfulness, wellness, and well-being.

Our character encapsulates our principles, values, ethics, and beliefs, serving as our inner power source. Regardless of our circumstances, positions, jobs, or roles in life, our character traits reflect our values, emotions, and choices, defining who we are and shaping our future. A person without a strong character is like a tall tree in a forest with very few leaves. Despite its height, the tree provides no shade or sustenance, ultimately not contributing to the forest. Similarly, living a directionless life without contribution or running away from responsibilities is akin to such a barren existence.

In my neighborhood, there was a remarkable student named Yadu who aspired to gain admission to a prestigious university. To achieve this goal, Yadu made significant sacrifices, abstaining from leisure activities, *and social events, and even reducing his sleep to a minimum. He devoted a year to intensive preparation, enrolling in a demanding coaching course and dedicating 16 hours a day to his studies. His unwavering commitment was evident in the dark circles under his eyes, a visual testament to his year-long struggle. Despite all his efforts, hard work, and powerful attempts, he could not clear his exam. Yadu's disappointment at not clearing the exam was deeply felt by those around him.*

It was quite surprising that all of Yadu's friends, who used to seek his help in clearing their doubts during preparation, had successfully gained admission to their favorite colleges. This left Yadu feeling overwhelmed with negative thoughts of being seen as a loser in the eyes of others. Yadu has been spending less time communicating with his parents, returning home late from his evening walk, and frequently having dinner late at night. Additionally, he tends to rise late in the morning and often becomes overly concerned about future events, allowing small issues to grow into lengthy complaints. Things seemed to be going from bad to worse for him. His father, noticing the change in Yadu's behavior, became concerned and started having nightmares about his son's well-being. He reached out to me to understand Yadu's current condition and ask for help to support his son in the best possible way.

When I spoke with Yadu, I inquired about his current activities, and he mentioned that he had made new friends and was enjoying their company. When I asked if he was now studying in groups, he explained that he still preferred self-study but spent his evenings with his new friends. I probed further about their evening activities, but he seemed hesitant to disclose any details despite my repeated inquiries. Then I asked him about his old friends, and how they cleared their exams when he could not pass. He expressed his belief that many of his friends had cheated to gain admission to their dream universities, despite seeking his help with their studies. He emphasized his commitment and dedication to his studies throughout the year, contrasting it with their attendance at social events and leisure activities. He firmly believed that his hard work made him more capable than his peers, and he was confident that he would succeed while maintaining his integrity. When I questioned the young boy once more, "Do you believe you can pass your examination on the second try?" He expressed his fear of failing the exam again. I asked why you think would fail when you are proficient in your studies and have prepared adequately. Yet, this time, he remained silent, unable to provide an answer.

Yadu, a brilliant student, is unknowingly grappling with internal turmoil. The insidious forces of stress and negativity have taken root within him, and courtesy of his self-importance, his tendency to view others as less capable and to consider himself superior has fostered a world of arrogance and egotism within him. His presumption kept Yadu under tremendous pressure during the examination. Being an academic champion, his desire to score the highest marks had made him nervous. After being inside for so long, with the feeling of being the best and the procrastination of being better than others, he had become prey to stress and negativity without realizing it. Now he has developed self-doubt, hindering him from performing better in any task. Despite his academic prowess, he must learn to be receptive to other perspectives to understand and act better against his internal turmoil.

As a virus corrupts a computer, pompous acts as a fuel to stress and negativity, weakening Yadu from within. We all know that in the world of computers, we have the option to utilize antivirus software to cleanse computer systems or seek assistance from skilled computer engineers who can identify and thwart any hacking attempts on our machines. Similarly, to purify and repel the influx of stress and negativity within us, we require a guide or a torch bearer to light our way out of the darkness.

After a while when I met Yadu, during a conversation with him, he confided in me about his struggles of accidentally falling for using drugs to cope with academic pressure and social stress. It seems like Yadu is struggling with a lot of internal and external pressures. He expressed a desire for a fresh start and a determination to pass his exams, it's commendable that he is willing to make a fresh start and clear his exams.

However, it's evident that he's facing internal battles that are impacting his well-being. It's important to address these issues with empathy and understanding. I advised him to identify his passions and reconnect with positive influences in his life. As Yadu's life was slipping into the dark world of Stress and Negativity, he must understand the impact of his negative thoughts and work towards making positive changes through Character Building.

INVISIBLE THREAD OF RULES:

Repetition often leads to boredom, and we thrive when we have the opportunity to experience new things. Imagine having the same bread for breakfast, lunch, and dinner every day. No one wants to eat the same thing repeatedly. Similarly, watching your all-time favorite movie every day for a year is unlikely. Change is a universal law of nature. We are naturally inclined to seek variety and change in our daily activities. Without change, life on earth would not exist. Our body is naturally designed to adapt to constant changes in nature. Our body is most active during the day and needs rest at night. This is a natural rhythm that applies to all human beings, our bodies are naturally equipped to handle these daily changes without any of our extra effort. As we are built to adapt to the world around us, why do we resist change when we are born to handle natural changes and those in our world? Our bodies change every second, yet we fear bad outcomes before trying something new. The key lies in understanding the universal law of change and its effectiveness, which we often overlook.

We witness these universal laws in the everyday transformation from day to night, sunsets giving way to moon and stars, and the transition from winter to summer.

Everything around us is in a constant state of change, from the blooming of a flower to the growth of a mighty tree. By delving into the universal law of change, we can uncover the profound truth beneath these transformations. These universal laws not only continuously alter everything around us but also preserve their unchanging natural core to remain effective and divine. This unyielding and unchanging natural core defines everything we perceive. The sun consistently rises in the east, and sets in the west, stars and the moon illuminate the night sky, fire is always hot while ice is perpetually cold, sugar is sweet and salt is salty, herbivores cannot consume meat and carnivores cannot subsist on grass. This unchanging natural core of nature serves to help us grasp the concept of the invisible thread of rule's importance. Our character is made from the invisible thread of unchanging rules and values. These rules and values are steadfast and cannot be altered to suit our convenience. As the sun will never rise from the west, stars will never shine during the day, fire will never be cold, ice will never be hot, sugar will never be salty, and salt will never be sweet. These unchangeable characteristics make the system of life eternal, as the universal law of change does not apply to their characteristics.

Similarly, we need to adhere to a fundamental set of unbreakable invincible rules that cannot be altered for our convenience. These invincible rules and core values form the unshakable foundation of our character, impervious to any future challenges or adversities. To build character, we must ignite the spark from within. By prioritizing our goals and dreams, we can gain the initial momentum to identify activities that bring us true happiness and satisfaction. This requires introspection to discover our unique interests and hobbies that resonate with our innermost joy and peace. This personal inventory is ours alone to create, as only we can truly understand the depth of our feelings and passions.

I encouraged Yadu to establish a rock-solid foundation for his character by honestly identifying his passions, driving forces, hobbies, favorite pastimes, and compassion. After much contemplation and discussion, he compiled a list. He expressed his love for watching the sunrise but lamented his inability to do so due to his long study hours and struggles with drugs. He also mentioned his passion for dancing, which he can no longer enjoy due to his weakened physical condition. Additionally, he expressed a desire to reconnect with his old friends and revealed that making his father smile at the dinner table is a major source of motivation for him. However, he has been isolating himself from family dinners due to his late nights spent with his new group of friends and their drug activities.

Yadu, once an ambitious, humble, courageous, honest, and loyal boy, has unfortunately succumbed to the negative influences of stress and negativity. These devils have caused a significant shift in his character, leading to an increased short temper, dishonesty in his studies, and a reluctance to face his family and old friends. Like many others, he has fallen victim to the perils of stress and negativity. It's a challenge that many of us face, and we often struggle to find the right path to overcome these obstacles. However, Yadu's resilience and honesty give hope that he will soon emerge from this darkness into a world of positivity. By focusing on building a strong character foundation, Yadu can pave his way to a brighter future. I strongly believe that pushing Yadu to create his own to-do list, which brings him genuine happiness and bliss, is the key to unlocking the limitless within. Instead of seeking external solutions or relying on others to solve his problems, he must compile a list of things that bring him peace, joy, and motivation. I *suggested that he jot down these things on paper and carry it with him, adding to it throughout the day. Then, he should prioritize and shorten the list, focusing on achievable goals within 24 hours.*

Developing a personalized plan becomes achievable when we devote our focus and energy to introspection, truly understanding ourselves, and identifying what brings us genuine happiness, positivity, and personal growth. It's crucial to emphasize that every item on this list must be deeply personal and relevant to us. Since nobody else can comprehend or experience our inner world the way we do, we alone have the power to act on our list. No external influence can bring us the peace and happiness we seek for our worthy life.

It's essential to create an achievable list to benefit and shape ourselves positively. Our top to-do list should be aligned with our inner peace. It's important to focus on realistic and attainable goals. By avoiding lofty or unattainable aspirations, we can build a strong foundation for our character. Our list should include tasks that truly resonate with us and are achievable within a reasonable timeframe. Let's keep our to-do list clear and straightforward, take time to reflect deeply, and connect with your innermost positive desires when creating this list.

YADU WEEK PLANNER

CHARACTER FOUNDATION	TRUST YOURSELF AND TAKE RESPONSIBILITY FOR FORMING A STRONG CHARACTER					
	MONDAY	TUESDAY	WEDNESDAY	THURSDAY	FRIDAY	SATURDAY	SUNDAY
SUNRISE	YES	YES	YES	YES	YES	YES	YES
DANCE CLASS	YES	YES	YES	YES	YES		
CALL A FRIEND	YES		YES		YES			
FAMILY DINNER	YES	YES		YES			YES
MOVIE TIME					YES		YES

Yadu is firmly committed to following this simple yet powerful plan for character-building and determined to make positive changes in his life. He has pledged to resist any temptation to take shortcuts or deviate from this plan. If he truly desires to secure admission to a top-tier college and lay the foundation for a successful future, he must wholeheartedly embrace each step. Yadu took a week to reflect on his life and made a vital realization: he was the source of his own problems. By focusing on activities that brought positivity into his life, he found himself better able to tackle challenges, stress, and negativity. Instead of doing drugs with new friends, he chose to spend quality time with his parents and ensure a good night's sleep so he could witness the sunrise the next day. Despite his difficulties initially in falling asleep, he managed to see the sunrise and even attended a dance class, despite feeling drained. Despite the temptation to do drugs with his new friends every evening, he stayed committed to his plan. He isn't indulging in his favorite activities excessively. Instead, he watches a movie twice a week, spends 15-20 minutes talking to friends 3 days a week, and attends a 5-day dance class at scheduled times. By engaging in these activities, he finds daily happiness and positivity within.

However, it's important to approach these activities with dedication and proper planning, rather than aimlessly. Spending quality time alone to reflect and discover our true selves is crucial for finding genuine happiness, peace, and positivity. After this introspection, we can incorporate these findings into our daily routine and wholeheartedly follow them. Though adhering to a daily plan may seem challenging at first, the initial struggle is worthwhile for a life filled with fulfillment and vast gains.

Yadu returned after a month, overcoming past mistakes, he realized the importance of focusing on his studies while still making time for the activities he loves. By embracing these activities, he found a renewed sense of joy and inner happiness. Yadu made a commitment to give up drugs and transform these activities into lifelong habits. He understood that our character is shaped by the rules and values we uphold and the habits we develop. He chose to leave behind negative influences, such as drugs, imaginary fears, and toxic company, while reconnecting with old friends and letting go of his ego.

Yadu discovered that his true character is not defined by negativity, but by the positive moments that bring joy to his life, like making his father smile, dancing to his favorite music, watching sci-fi movies, and witnessing the sunrise each morning. Yadu discovered something extraordinary in activities he once considered futile, prompting him to let go of his old habits. He realized that true happiness and prosperity come from within, rather than external possessions or pursuits. It's important to focus on our own values and not rely on external role models for guidance. Just as giving something valuable to a person in need elicits generosity in return, prioritizing positive habits over negative ones can lead to an extravagant lifestyle that prevents us from falling prey to stress and negativity.

After solidifying his foundation and diligently following the 5 natural laws, Yadu successfully passed his examinations on his second attempt and gained admission to one of the top technical universities in the country. This achievement filled his parents and friends with pride. Yadu's commitment to his daily routine, which may seem simple but is deeply ingrained in his character, kept him on the right path and shielded him from the stress and negativity that threatened to steer him astray. His experience demonstrates how embracing positivity and strong values can help overcome the adversities of everyday life.

TRUE TO-DO LIST

For instance, when selecting fruit and vegetables, we always choose the best pieces available, just as we avoid buying rotten produce. Similarly, we should be equally selective about the habits we adopt. If a habit or activity gives off negative vibes, it's best to steer clear, even if it seems appealing at first. These negative influences can gradually erode our well-being, leading to stress and negativity. Just as we protect our devices from unsafe elements, we must safeguard our peace, happiness, and positivity by steering clear of detrimental habits. Strengthening our character requires us to embrace positive values and habits that bring us inner peace and wisdom.

Negative thoughts hinder our personal growth and prevent us from achieving our full potential. When negative thoughts discourage us from making to-do lists and provide countless reasons why this won't benefit us, it's important to recognize that time alone will not heal or bring about positive change. Many people tend to procrastinate when it comes to pursuing their dreams or reaching the pinnacle of success. However, those who only procrastinate will never succeed and will continue to endure a life filled with challenges and hardships. These individuals are unable to overcome their struggles and eventually give up on their dreams, resigning themselves to a life of difficulty and adversity. We encounter such individuals daily.

If we want to achieve our life's dreams, we must believe in a self-designed system of principles to cultivate a resilient and unbeatable character, capable of facing and conquering life's challenges, stress, and negativity. Crafting a personalized and impactful list of laws is a straightforward endeavor. The key is simple: honesty. Take a moment to delve deep within and consider the natural elements, tasks, habits, hobbies, and activities that truly resonate with you. Ensure that your to-do list of laws is comprised of activities that genuinely bring you joy, positivity, and inner peace.

If we're struggling to create a to-do list that truly resonates with us and empowers us, it's important to consider the influence of our inner dialogue. Our minds can either work for us or against us. By harnessing the positive aspects of our thinking, we can generate a powerful to-do list that contributes to our personal growth. Taking a step-by-step approach and acknowledging both our weaknesses and strengths will guide us to a successful and fulfilling life. It's essential to jot down all our capabilities, regardless of the quantity, on paper as a first step towards constructing a strong character and filtering them.

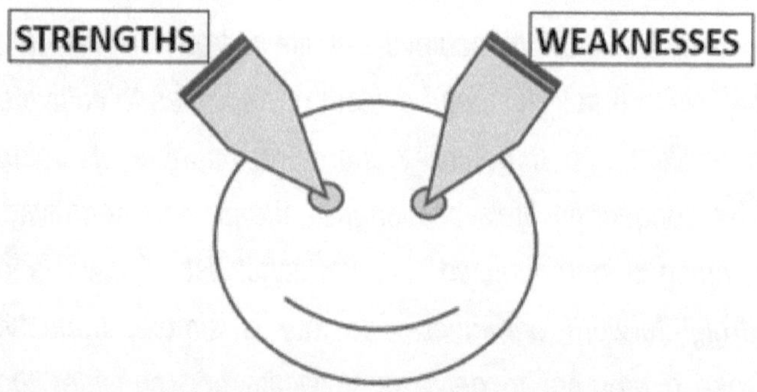

Once we have identified our strengths and weaknesses, we must align them with our life goals. Without a clear

aim, our potential remains untapped, causing us to become complacent. Whether it's gaining admission to a top college, excelling in exams, securing a job, advancing in our career, or expanding our business, our goals should guide the way we assess our strengths and weaknesses. It's important to note that this information shouldn't be discarded but rather retained for future reference, with ongoing updates as we pursue new goals and endeavors.

Once we've identified our strengths and weaknesses, it's crucial to embed them into our mindset in order to prioritize them in our daily tasks. We must constantly remind ourselves of our strengths and use them as a source of confidence, reinforcing our belief in our abilities. This self-esteem will be the catalyst for improving our weaknesses. Step by step, we should strategize on how to tackle each weakness. If addressing our weaknesses calls for training, guidance, or coaching, we must promptly seek out suitable resources and enroll. Once enrolled, it's our responsibility to wholeheartedly commit to the plan with utmost sincerity. Similarly, we should add any necessary skill-building or learning efforts to our to-do list, aligning with our life goals to fortify our character effectively.

Engaging in physical activities such as gym, yoga, swimming, running, jogging, cycling, boxing, meditation, cricket, tennis, football, basketball, volleyball, etc. in the early morning at 4 or 5 AM can significantly boost your energy levels throughout the day. Physical strength and mental fortitude are essential to sustain these activities, but as you progress, the effort required diminishes. Typically, results become noticeable after 15 days or by the third week, and after a month of consistency, you'll find yourself fully immersed in the transformative process. Just one month of commitment can kickstart your journey towards achieving your life goals. Waiting indefinitely for things to happen will only lead to perpetual struggle and misery. To break free and make significant strides, we need to plan, filter, and steadfastly adhere to our principles of success.

My colleague's son, Prateet, recently opened up to me about his current situation. Despite holding a degree, he's working at a call centre and is determined to change his future for the better. He's surrounded by friends who are excelling in their careers, and he's ready to make a big change in his life. Despite not focusing on his studies in college and getting involved with the wrong crowd, Prateet is now motivated to make up for lost time and create a successful future for himself. His determination and passion to improve his life were clear during our conversation. He's contemplating returning to track but seeks more clarity on how to proceed.

I encouraged Prateet to pursue a course that aligns with his aspirations for the next 5 to 10 years. He expressed his ambition to become a general manager in a large organization, exuding tremendous confidence and a positive attitude. I explained that to achieve this goal, he would need a business degree from a reputable college or relevant experience along with notable recognition and strong references. While currently lacking these qualifications, I assured him that it's possible to attain them in the coming years. I outlined two options: pursuing a management program to secure a job at a reputable organization, and the second option is to actively applying for positions related to his current degree and gradually working towards his dream role.

I advised him to approach life with the mindset of a general manager, focusing on productivity and discipline. Wasting time on social media or leisurely activities would not align with his goals. I stressed the importance of character development and leveraging his positive energy to overcome weaknesses and adhere to 5 natural laws.

Furthermore, I recommended studying the teachings of Swami Vivekananda for inspiration. He acknowledged my advice and departed with his father.

A while back, I got a call from Prateet. He was thrilled to share that he had just earned a business degree from LBS in London and had received multiple job offers from top organizations. He credited his success to working on his character and understanding the 5 natural laws with utmost honesty and commitment, which he believes have unlocked immense potential within himself. With clear aspirations of becoming the youngest General Manager in a Fortune 100 company, he is now planning to relocate his parents to London. His story serves as a powerful reminder that with the right mindset and unwavering determination, anyone can overcome challenges and achieve their life goals.

Visualizing how our lives will dramatically change, living in a grand mansion, driving a luxury sports car, excelling in our endeavors, enjoying worry-free vacations with our loved ones, and living a life of abundance, can ignite our motivation and drive. These aspirations will guide us in achieving our life goals and will help us overcome stress and negativity. During our journey to build our character, we must confront and conquer our inner thoughts of failure. Thoughts of failure will constantly tempt us to disregard the rules, take a break, and procrastinate. They will try to convince us that we have plenty of time and that everything will miraculously improve. These thoughts will persist and grow stronger if we entertain them. It is crucial to pay attention to our thoughts of success during this time.

To succeed in life, it's crucial to challenge ourselves. Without determination and pushing our limits, achieving our goals is impossible. Life entails daily struggles such as nourishment, clothing, and shelter. These necessities require hard work and perseverance to obtain. Some individuals possess innate strengths or develop traits that make acquiring these essentials less demanding. However, character development is a one-time, honest, and serious undertaking. Our character holds the key to unlocking a world of endless possibilities by directing our focus towards positivity. Once we tap into this ocean of optimism, everything falls into place, and our body and mind can accurately predict future outcomes. This wellspring of positivity resides within every human being, but it's only accessible to those who channel their focus within and embrace it.

To design our character effectively, it's crucial to keep

our to-do list private and strictly adhere to it. By prioritizing the disciplined execution of our tasks, we can avoid self-deception. While it may take time to plan and integrate these activities into our daily schedules, staying committed and honest in the initial stages is key. Despite the challenges and initial discomfort, sticking to our to-do list is essential. Creating a simple plan with realistic timings is the path to success. It's important to avoid overloading ourselves with an unachievable list and instead focus on a few manageable tasks. Remember, this journey is an internal one that requires self-reliance and determination. No external support can replace the conviction and honesty needed for character building. Just as no one can eat or digest food for us, no one can undertake this journey on our behalf.

When we embark on the journey of shaping our character, we often encounter challenges that threaten to disrupt our progress. It's easy to find reasons to avoid working on our character-building in the beginning. However, we must confront these distractions and push back against negative thoughts that may deter us from completing our journey. Even when motivation is lacking, it's essential to remain engaged and focused on achieving our goals. Once we commit to character-building, we must adopt a mindset of perseverance, refusing to entertain thoughts of giving up. There's no room for excuses or setbacks in this journey. We must wholeheartedly dedicate ourselves to this process, recognizing that character-building is essential for future endeavors. Selfishness, in this context, is beneficial as we prioritize our development. We must consistently seek ways to adhere to our plans, ensuring that character-building takes precedence over all other tasks.

A person's character plays a vital role in their internal journey towards positivity. A negative character can be a major obstacle to achieving positivity. Individuals with a bad character tend to be dishonest with themselves, making it difficult to be honest with others or accomplish their goals. On the other hand, an ethical and honest character serves as a reliable companion, helping individuals tackle challenges during their internal journey. It's essential to have a strong character by our side to navigate difficult times and stay true to our path. Make sure your list of rules and values reflects your internal connection, not external influences. It's important that these personal guidelines are for your eyes and ears only. Avoid seeking validation or showing off. Your focus should be on shaping your character for yourself, not for others. Engaging in these activities will allow you to experience genuine joy, happiness, peace, and positivity. By following the invisible thread of rules, we can tap into the abundant natural positive energies of the universe, radiating positive energy through our character. A strong and ethical character serves as a reliable friend, guiding us through challenges and preventing us from faltering during difficult times. Conversely, a weak character can lead us to deceive ourselves and others, hindering our progress. Therefore, nurturing a strong and honest character is crucial for success and resilience in our internal journey.

It's important to recognize that no matter how hard we try, we can't always persuade others to see things from our perspective. Instead of expending our energy on seeking external validation, we should focus on our internal journey toward positivity and self-improvement. By prioritizing our well-being and working to eliminate stress and negativity from within, we can achieve lasting results. The power of these invincible threads lies in their invisibility, discussing them outside dilutes their impact and may lead to unexpected consequences. Instead, we should focus on internalizing our feelings and harnessing positive energy from the universe. Sharing our invisible *threads with others is akin to wasting our energy, like vomiting instead of digesting and benefiting from it. When we flaunt or disclose our plans for character development, our focus and attention are diverted outward, disrupting our energy flow. Let's direct our energy inward for a more impactful and fulfilling transformation.*

When we shop for clothes, shoes, or other wearable items, we are often drawn to well-known brands. This is because brands provide us with a sense of reliability and quality. We trust that these companies produce high-quality products and prioritize customer satisfaction. We choose specific brands because we are familiar with their consistent quality and value for money. Some brands stay in fashion, while others innovate and stay fresh. These are all examples of how brands instill confidence in our purchasing decisions. Similarly, building a strong character gives us a sense of fulfillment, peace, and self-confidence. A robust character helps us stay focused on our goals and avoid aimless wandering.

During my professional career, I used to meet with construction heads at project sites to present our solutions for simplifying their construction processes and execution. I was overseeing two industrial projects at that time. In one of the project sites of a tire manufacturing plant, I had the opportunity to meet Mr. Toshiko, a Japanese national who was the construction head. At another project site of the FMCG industrial plant, I had the opportunity to meet with Mr. Nile, who was heading the site. I had excellent working relationships with both Mr. Toshiko and Mr. Nile. These projects started simultaneously and had similar project values and completion timelines of approximately 10 months. My meetings with Mr. Nile were often unplanned and unscheduled, typically conducted in his air-conditioned office. On the contrary, my meetings with Mr. Toshiko were always planned, and he predominantly preferred hands-on demonstrations of the solutions I suggested, often at the project site. Both industrial plants adopted and implemented the construction solutions recommended by my company, which made their project processes and operations more efficient and faster, saving time without compromising construction quality.

One morning, Mr. Toshiko and I had a scheduled meeting at 9:30. While we were talking, Mr. Toshiko received a message about a machine operator getting injured and his machine malfunctioning. Without hesitation and delay, Mr. Toshiko, dressed in his bright white shirt, rushed to the construction site, and I followed.

When we arrived, we saw the injured operator receiving first aid while the machine continued to run erratically. No one was willing to approach the machine to stop it. Mr. Toshiko quickly assessed the situation, leaped onto the machine, and managed to stop it. He then ensured the operator's well-being and swiftly resumed our meeting, prompting me to present potential solutions right where we had left off, despite getting his white shirt covered in grease stains. On the other hand, Mr. Nile always maintains impeccably neat, clean, and well-ironed clothes while delegating work to his juniors and primarily working from his air-conditioned chamber. Mr. Toshiko's admirable character inspired loyalty and teamwork at his site, whereas Mr. Nile's construction site was plagued by politics and time-wasting activities. As a result, the tire plant finished ahead of schedule, while the FMCG plant faced numerous operational challenges and fell behind. This shows that strong character and ethics are essential for achieving our goals and meeting targets in every aspect of life.

Everyone in our social circle and neighborhood aspires to achieve a better and more prosperous life. But what sets apart those who attain this lifestyle? We can gain valuable insights by learning from the success stories of individuals who have achieved significant wealth. These individuals enjoy grand homes, luxury cars, and sizable bank accounts, all with minimal concerns about future challenges. I recently had a fascinating conversation with a stock market investor and was intrigued by their experiences with market fluctuations and trends. I gained a deep appreciation for the excitement and allure of the stock market. This individual's passion for trading and understanding stocks was truly admirable, and their substantial earnings reflected their dedication. When I asked about their secret, they revealed that they had established a set of personal rules and never deviated from them. By adhering to these principles daily, they were able to thrive, even amidst occasional losses. Rules govern every aspect of our lives, and those who live under their own established guidelines, following them wholeheartedly, find that achieving success becomes straightforward. Even the most complex challenges in life become more manageable and attainable for those who live by their self-imposed rules.

In any sport or game, victory belongs to the player who understands and abides by the rules. Physical strength and mental acuity are important, but adherence *to the rules and game plan is crucial for success. Those who disregard the rules often find themselves on the losing end. To attain personal or familial success, honesty and careful planning are essential. We must nurture our character through positive, attainable tasks, aligning our mind, body, and soul. By prioritizing our goals and envisioning a bright future, we can fortify ourselves against negativity. character through positive, attainable tasks, aligning our mind, body, and soul. By prioritizing our goals and envisioning a bright future, we can fortify ourselves against negativity.*

Understanding the importance of invisible threads of rules to develop our character is crucial and can be an enjoyable activity. By honestly working on developing our character, we will experience a positive change within ourselves. These invisible threads of rules will fortify our strong and true character and empower us to stand tall, strong, and effective throughout our lives, attracting worldly success naturally. It is crucial to build our character without being swayed by external influences. Our social circles may resist change, but the drive for change should come from within. We must remain steadfast in our practice, regardless of others' opinions. External opinions can draw us deeper into a metaphorical bog. To overcome this, we need a positive attitude and strong character to combat the challenges of this era. Resisting stress and negativity becomes easier when we tap into our internal source of positivity and strength.

It is crucial to adhere to ethical standards when developing our character. Deceiving ourselves with unfulfilled promises undermines our ability to live honestly and authentically. We must be truthful and genuine with ourselves before we can demonstrate honesty and authenticity to others. Our journey toward honesty and authenticity begins within us. Upholding ethical and moral values is essential for building character and achieving success in line with the 5 natural laws. To establish our own set of personal guiding principles, we must take inventory of our preferences, aspirations, driving forces, and passions. These are the sources of our inner peace, joy, and illumination. Instead of seeking external sources or external validation, we should direct our focus and energy inward. Solitude provides the ideal setting for deep introspection. We must ponder independently on questions such as: What have I been drawn to since childhood? What fuels my motivation? What activities bring me joy? What lifts my spirit? Reflecting on these questions in solitude can help us uncover our core values, principles, and true to-do list.

 Without developing our character, we are susceptible to stress and negativity as we search for external solutions, only to realize that true success comes from within. A person without a strong character will struggle to make the right decisions. When our character does not align with our internal values and happiness, our judgments become uncertain. Conflicting views on what is right and wrong can lead to confusion in life's complexities. Once we establish a robust character based on our values and principles, we gain confidence and commitment to our chosen path, free from the distractions of the external world. By anchoring ourselves with personal rules, principles, and values, we simplify life's complexities and stay true to our realities. Building a strong character is crucial in overcoming stress and negativity and understanding 5 natural laws.

Once, a saint was walking near a river and spotted a drowning scorpion. The saint entered the river and rescued the scorpion, but was stung in the process. The scorpion fell back into the water, but the saint rescued it again, only to be stung once more. Despite the stings, the saint persisted in saving the scorpion's life. A bystander asked the saint why he continued to save the scorpion *despite being stung. The saint calmly explained that it was in his character to save life, just as it was in the scorpion's character to sting. Both were true to their inherent character and couldn't change. The story of the saint and the scorpion is a compelling illustration of the significance of character in our lives. Despite being stung repeatedly, the saint remained resolute in his determination to save the scorpion. This unwavering commitment to doing what is morally right, even in the face of adversity, serves as a powerful example of the importance of staying true to one's character. It's a poignant reminder of the resilience and fortitude that comes from embracing inner peace and maintaining a positive and steadfast character, especially when confronted with obstacles, stress, and negativity in our lives.*

CHAPTER 2
<u>SECOND NATURAL LAW - RECENTMENT</u>

Resentment is a powerful ally and a powerhouse that fuels stress and negativity inside us. Although stress and negativity may not attack until they gain strength from resentment during our moments of weakness. It is important to recognize that stress and negativity do not have inherent power but this is us who allow them to become stronger by succumbing to resentment. When we let resentment take control, we feel powerless against the web of dark thoughts.

We have all heard countless stories of long-time best friends, family members, cousins, business partners, and colleagues turning against each other over minor issues or in fits of rage. While unfortunate events may occur in relationships or lives, allowing a peaceful mind to turn into a criminal or a murderer in a fit of rage should never be an acceptable outcome. There are many rules and laws in *place to combat unfair practices and fight for justice. However, the question remains: to what extent is it justified to take those laws into our own hands? Our world is in a much darker time than ever before with numerous horrible incidents like mass killings, school shootings, mall shootings, market shootings, music fest shootings, and religious gathering shootings in recent years leaving us all in a bombshell of grief. Do you not feel that the spilling of innocent blood has become cheaper than buying our everyday grocery items nowadays? Who is responsible for what is happening around us? Are we all responsible? Despite living in an era of open information and technology that can improve human lives, why do we still harbor so much anger, hate, and annoyance? It's highly likely that the person sitting next to us, living next door, working with us, or flying with us is struggling with anger management or resentment. In this era, human life seems cheaper than ever before. We must break free from these destructive forces and reclaim our inner strength.*

Once there were two brothers who worked hard to support their family by selling snacks outside a liquor shop along with their father since childhood. Despite facing numerous challenges in their early lives, they eventually found success by starting their shop, expanding the business to more shops, and even owning public transport. After years of hardships and commitments, they further grew their wealth through wise investments in real estate, their net worth reached millions. However, after their father's passing, disputes over property and assets arose, leading to a tragic end for both brothers. The brothers managed to settle all their conflicts, except for the dispute over their family home. Despite their considerable wealth, they were at odds over a small piece of land that belonged to their old house. This disagreement escalated to the point where they eventually agreed to meet one evening in a parking lot to address the matter. In a fit of rage, both brothers fired several shots at each other and both died on the spot. The tragic loss of both brothers resulted in their mother being left alone with substantial wealth in the bank and valuable properties. With the sudden passing of her sons, she sadly succumbed to a cardiac arrest within six months. This devastating turn of events left nothing but an inheritance for the family, wiping out the years of struggle and hardship endured by the parents and their children. This resentment took everything from them after years of struggle and hard work. The resulting loss and sorrow serve as a stark reminder of the destructive force of resentment.

Many times, in the heat of discussion or argument, we tend to pass judgment without considering the facts. We often jump to conclusions and make decisions without giving the other person a chance to speak. Where is our capacity for forgiveness? Have we lost faith in the higher power that governs the universe? Do we truly want to control everything according to our desires? No one is inherently a criminal, killer, or saint. It is our environment, perspectives, and choices that shape us into who we become. Our inner thoughts and emotions, such as happiness, frustration, resentment, and the desire for revenge, accompany us everywhere we go. Sometimes, we are unaware of our inner selves and our true feelings. Without realizing it, we become immersed in feelings of resentment and become victims of anger. If we seek guidance and understanding, we can save ourselves from falling into the darkness of destructive desires and emotions before it's too late.

It's within our control to prevent resentment from overpowering us and causing us harm. We have the power to overcome our inner struggles and turn them into opportunities. Many people have already done this, serving as examples for us to follow. We can choose the right path and make the correct decisions, and many inspiring individuals around us can guide us toward positivity and hope. It's important to recognize that resentment is a major source of stress and negativity, and we must overcome it to shine and thrive.

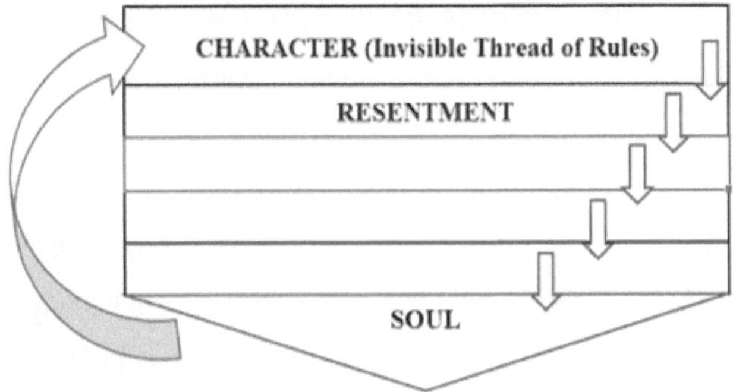

Do we want to surround ourselves with individuals who constantly pick fights over trivial matters or incessantly engage in unnecessary arguments? The answer is clear - we all desire the presence of loving, honest, caring, thoughtful, and responsible individuals in our lives. While disagreements are inevitable, they are a natural part of human interaction. No two lives are identical, and variations in opinions and preferences are to be expected. Embracing these differences is essential for a harmonious coexistence.

Sometimes one person must yield, while at other times, the other must yield to keep the gears turning in family relationships, business endeavors, and friendships. However, this delicate balance can only be maintained when neither party is afflicted and overpowered with the resentment ailment. If the other person never yields, never agrees to your needs, disregards your feelings, and slips out of your control, the situation quickly spirals out of control and we all know where this leads. Typically, relationships disintegrate, business empires crumble, and friends turn into enemies. The power of resentment can transform a stable situation into chaos in an instant. A once joyful life turns bleak, a thriving business collapses, and lifelong friends become sworn enemies. Stress and negativity drain our inner positivity and can ruin lives in mere seconds. The powerhouse of resentment is a force that most people struggle to control. It traps us in feelings of rage, anger, and agony, allowing stress and negativity to take over our thoughts. This negativity often leads to dangerous and regrettable actions, such as road rage incidents and senseless violence.

STING OF RESENTMENT

Once there lived a tribe woman who went to the nearby

market to procure essential items for her home. The tribe woman left her one-year-old child sleeping in the cradle with her loyal dog. While she was away, a large snake from the nearby jungle slithered into the child's room. The loyal dog quickly sprang into action, attacking the snake. After a fierce fight, the dog successfully killed the snake and threw it into a corner of the room. The commotion woke the child, who began to cry. When the tribe woman came back, she heard her child's cries, and the tribe woman rushed back into her baby's room. She discovered her dog with blood smeared all over its face and noticed blood stains spread throughout the room. In her absence, she thought the dog had bitten her baby, prompting her to grab an axe. Despite the loyal dog's friendly approach, she killed it in a fit of rage. Upon checking her baby, she found no signs of injury but discovered a dead snake nearby. It dawned on her that she had mistakenly killed her loyal dog, who had actually saved her baby from the snake. She now deeply regrets her impulsive actions but knows that what's done is done.

Decisions made out of resentment are never trustworthy or beneficial. They often lead to a destructive path, even affecting the most brilliant minds. We have seen countless stories of individuals taking matters into *their own hands in fits of anger, resulting in irreversible damage to their lives. This dark force of resentment can cause individuals to harm others or themselves, suppressing their positive qualities and leading to tragic outcomes. Lives are lost, families are torn apart, and individuals end up imprisoned, filled with regret for their impulsive actions. It's time to disentangle ourselves from this destructive cycle that yields power to stress and negativity. It is essential to break free from the control of resentment and embrace our brighter, positive thoughts to make life-affirming decisions.*

Another insidious effect of stress and negativity is the way it can lead us to resent those who are hardworking and successful. What starts as a small sense of dislike can quickly grow into a consuming jealousy, driving us to wish ill upon others. Instead of focusing on self-improvement and personal growth, we become fixated on the downfall of others. These destructive thoughts drain us of positivity and cloud our judgment, leading us down a path of self-ruin. It's important to remember that harboring ill will towards others only leads to our own downfall.

When one of my friends, Avi, and some other recruits joined a multinational company in a junior position, after completing five years in the organization, he found his colleagues advanced in their careers and reached senior positions, while he was stuck in the same position. He came to me and described how all his colleagues, who he believes are equally competent and hardworking, had received promotions and were now leading major teams despite achieving lower annual results. He expressed disappointment in the company's potentially non-merit-based promotion and reward system and felt demoralized by the unfair treatment. He questioned why his bosses had not allowed him to grow professionally or lead larger teams. I advised him to focus on enhancing his skills rather than attributing blame to his bosses or colleagues. I also suggested that if the situation didn't improve, he should consider pursuing opportunities elsewhere that would recognize his contributions and provide a fairer work environment. However, he expressed his determination to continue fighting against the unfair treatment by his bosses.

After a while, I ran into Avi at a local saloon. He told me that he had been fired by the company because of a physical altercation with his boss. He seemed to have given up on the corporate world, blaming his shortcomings on others and the negative environment. I knew him as a bright student since my childhood and his behavior was never like this. It was clear to me that he was battling inner resentment, which was overshadowing his true potential and character. If he had recognized this and worked on overcoming his resentment, his life could have taken a different turn toward a more positive and better path.

The pervasive influence of stress and negativity has deeply impacted families worldwide. The rise of nuclear families can be attributed to a lack of understanding and compatibility among family members. Parents feel misunderstood by their children, while siblings feel the same about their parents. This insidious influence leads to separation and conflict within families, stemming from minor disagreements to intense and prolonged discord. Parents, who have dedicated their lives to their children, often feel unappreciated and neglected. Despite the sacrifices and efforts made, they perceive a lack of care, respect, and agreement from their children, which leads to emotional distress and separation.

It's important to recognize that when siblings also experience high levels of stress and negativity, their situation can be just as challenging as that of their parents or elders in the family. Children may struggle with negative thoughts, and feel unappreciated despite *investing significant time and effort into their education or professional lives to provide for their families. This shared burden can lead to family members drifting apart, with little desire to reconnect, even in critical moments. Is this truly the natural way to live or to bid farewell to one another, especially within our own family or in our bloodline?*

In my sophomore year of college, I encountered a student named Iqbal who had failed his second-year exams and was held back. I noticed that he kept to himself and seemed reserved. Despite his reluctance to share, I reached out to him to learn about his background and experiences. While Iqbal didn't fully open up, I sensed that he was struggling with feelings of isolation and disappointment. I recognized the impact of his situation and felt compelled to offer my support. Iqbal was a reserved individual, not particularly inclined towards technical studies. Nonetheless, he displayed remarkable discipline by adhering to his college schedule. Despite his dedicated efforts, he unfortunately did not succeed in passing the exam that year. As we progressed to the 3rd year, Iqbal remained in the 2nd year, exuding a perpetually serious demeanor. He could often be found in the library, his hostel room, or in the mess during our meal times.

I usually make an effort to engage in conversations with him, but he typically responds briefly before retreating to his room or the library. One late night, there was a knock at my door. When I opened it, I was surprised to find Iqbal standing there. He had never visited my room in the last two years. Iqbal asked if I had some time and requested that I join him outside. He held a laboratory experiment file and asked for my assistance with one of the experiments. I focused intently, guiding him through the experiment. After thanking me, he opened up about his struggles to pass the exam and how this technical program didn't seem to be his calling. He shared that both of his parents held prominent positions in government services and it was their dream for him to complete this technical program. He admitted that his parents wouldn't want him to return home without finishing his degree. Despite the weight of his words, he smiled as he shared his personal information with me. I had never seen him smile, but I was hopeful that by unburdening himself, he would feel lighter. I assured him that he would definitely pass the exam this year. "Not much is going to change this year, too," he said, smiling. He then left, expressing gratitude for taking up my time. I assured him that it was not a problem and encouraged him to visit and talk to me anytime.

The next morning, I didn't see Iqbal in the college mess for breakfast, which was unusual as I usually saw him during those times. On my way back to my hostel room, I noticed a group of students gathered outside the boys' hostel building, whispering to each other. When I inquired about the commotion, one of the boys told me the shocking news that Iqbal had died by suicide. I was in disbelief, as I had seen him just the night before, his smiling face fresh in my memory. It was difficult to accept that he had taken such a drastic step. One of my classmates also showed up. He approached me and said, "Can you believe Iqbal did that?" I heard my classmate's voice while still having Iqbal's smiling face fresh in my mind. I replied, "He came to my room for the first time yesterday night after all these years and met me. If I had known he would do this, I could have supported him." My classmate mentioned that Iqbal had met a few other students yesterday, including me. Perhaps he wanted to meet a few of us for the last time, maybe he felt something inside. We came to know that Iqbal had been under tremendous pressure from his parents and had been facing continuous resentment and neglect from them. He couldn't bear this pressure and took this extreme step.

Iqbal's parents arrived at the hospital mortuary the following morning to claim the body of their only son. Their relentless push for him to succeed in a technical course had tragically cost them their beloved child. They never anticipated that their son would take such a drastic step. I witnessed his father in tears, lamenting that had Iqbal confided in them, they could have brought him back home and fulfilled his dreams of owning a business, hotel, restaurant, or shop. Iqbal's parents were unaware of his struggles, having prohibited him from coming home even during holidays until he passed his exams.

Iqbal's life teaches us that parents are the ultimate source of love, positivity, and motivation for their children. It's undeniable that parents make endless sacrifices and endure hardships to ensure their children have better lives and fulfill their dreams. While it's important for parents to dream big and set ambitious goals for their kids, but kids alone can't achieve greatness on their own. Parents play a crucial role in guiding, motivating, and unconditionally loving their children. Parents need to understand their children's strengths, and weaknesses, and support them during challenging times. Balancing *gentle pressure, appropriate discipline, and unwavering love is key to nurturing children effectively. Love is the most powerful motivation for our loved ones, and nothing can replace the love that parents have for their children.*

It's important to remember that being stuck in a circle of resentment can never bring any good to anyone. Just like how water held at a certain place starts to stink, harboring resentment only breeds negativity. On the other hand, allowing fresh thoughts to flow into our lives can keep us feeling fresh and free from negativity. Resentment traps us in a negative cycle of thoughts and obstructs the flow of positivity into our lives. Our inner positive thoughts often urge us to break free from the circle of resentment and live life to the fullest, but we tend to ignore them. We can learn from other people's lives and experiences, and take control over our resentment. By striving to find our positive signals and reintroducing peace and love into our lives, we can take firm steps to remove stress and negativity.

Resentment leads us down a dark path, causing the rupture of relationships, breeding negative thoughts, and inciting harmful actions. When negativity takes hold, it blinds us to reason, leading to senseless incidents and fatal consequences, it leads us away from positivity, severs our relationships, and plunges us into a realm of negativity. Often, this negativity dictates our thoughts without us even realizing it. Consider the everyday occurrences of road rage. It's astounding how two strangers can become completely consumed by anger over trivial matters. We frequently hear about fatal incidents triggered by reckless driving, unnecessary fighting, and fatal competition for dominance on the road. It's only when we find ourselves isolated behind bars that we truly understand the extent of our actions. We long for the company of loved ones and dearly miss the good moments of life. Sadly, we cannot undo the irreversible damage caused by our outbursts, resulting in irreparable loss and regret. Let's break free from this cycle of destruction and choose peace over conflict.

Can we make our world better by shutting down the powerhouse that fuels stress and negativity? Is it even worth celebrating and enjoying life if we cannot share our joy, achievements, and high points with our loved ones? Should we close the doors of resentment and never let it back in our magnificent lives, to preserve our close and meaningful relationships? Think about it – without resentment, we can stay together, avoid separation, prevent financial losses, and find our true inner peace, calmness, and love for everyone around us. Even animals stick together in their pride, leap, band, herds, tribes, strings, and groups. As the superior, smarter, and more intelligent species on this planet, it's only natural that we should do the same. We must find a way to free ourselves from the grip of stress and negativity.

CIRCLE OF POSITIVE & NEGATIVE THOUGHT SIGNALS

The key to shutting down resentment lies in seizing our positive thoughts. While it may be challenging at first, it gets easier with practice. When faced with resentment, our minds often gravitate towards negative thoughts, overshadowing our true positive nature. In moments of impulse, our minds send us alternating signals - one positive and the other negative. These signals persist throughout our discussions or conversations. It's up to us to choose which signal to listen to and act upon, shaping the course of our thoughts and conversations. Even after choosing one signal, the other remains, persistently vying for attention. This creates a circular or closed-loop pattern in our thinking.

Virtually all of us are familiar with the weight of life's struggles. From our first cry as newborns to the relentless pursuit of security and success, the journey is fraught with challenges. It's no wonder that negativity often takes root in our minds, given the constant battle to overcome obstacles. However, it's crucial that we consciously steer our thoughts toward positivity. By doing so, we can create a more fulfilling and meaningful existence, despite the adversities we may face.

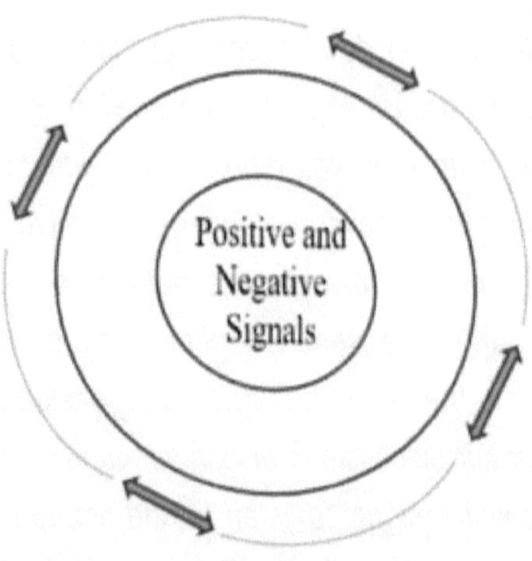

Choosing to follow a positive signal in life can set us on the right course and lead to a successful and better life. We can maintain the right course and end our discussions on a high note. However, negative signals

often creep in, disrupting the positive flow and planting seeds of doubt in our minds. We've all witnessed or experienced situations where someone initially remained composed but suddenly became aggressive and lost control. When asked about their behavior, they often admit to not understanding what came over them. I am sure many of us can relate having found ourselves in a similar situation where we acted strangely without understanding. It's a common experience to fall for negative signals even after recognizing the right path. So, how can we prevent making mistakes in such situations?

During military missions, troops must remain calm and positive to make the right decisions and follow the correct signals. Recruits must be wary of falling prey to negative signals, as acting on them during combat can have dire consequences. These negative signals may falsely project courage and independence, leading individuals to act alone rather than as part of a team. Disregarding orders in favor of negative signals leaves no room for second chances in life-threatening situations. It is essential to recognize and hold on to positive signals, regardless of how the mind may forecast future outcomes. As we approach the end of our metaphorical boxing match against resentment, we must learn to be unwavering in our commitment to positive signals. To avoid serious consequences such as legal trouble, damaged relationships, or financial loss, it is crucial to identify and follow our positive signals. Despite the persistent negative signals that may cause confusion or false hope, it is essential to remain committed to our positive signal throughout any situation or conversation. Always keep in mind that positive signals have the power to bring calm, positivity, relaxation, brightness, and peace to our bodies and minds. On the contrary, negative signals prompt us to act hastily, impulsively, and aggressively.

This is not to say that we should not embody qualities such as assertiveness, boldness, and competitiveness. It is important to carry these traits with us, but the timing of when to utilize them is crucial. In the event of an attack with a sharp weapon in a public place, it's crucial to remember that our instinctual signals play a significant role in our response. The positive signal urges us to act swiftly and decisively to protect ourselves, while the negative signal may cause us to freeze and hope for the best. Choosing to heed the positive signal means taking proactive and assertive actions to ensure our safety, such as finding a way to escape or arming ourselves with nearby objects for self-defense. It's important to resist the negative thoughts that may arise and instead focus on staying aware and seeking assistance from others if possible. By acknowledging and countering our negative signals, we can empower ourselves to respond effectively in dangerous situations.

If we encounter humiliation, discrimination, or victimization in any situation of life, our positive signal urges us to be bold, courageous, and assertive, while our negative thoughts may push us to remain silent and timid. It's important to identify and follow our positive signals to navigate such situations effectively. Catching onto positive signals initiates a journey of positivity and calmness within our minds, which is reflected in our actions. On the other hand, becoming entangled in resentment leads us into a realm of darkness, where stress and negativity reign. resentment offers no value, whereas the vast power of positivity and positive thoughts resides within us, enabling us to navigate any adversity. Let's commit to distancing ourselves from the destructive force of resentment, preserving the tranquillity of our lives.

TUNE IN FOR THE POSITIVE THOUGHT SIGNAL

One time, my family and I were on our way to a hill station, and my wife was behind the wheel. She is an extremely careful driver who always adheres to the rules of the road. During our journey, another car rear-ended us at a high speed. The impact caused our jeep to veer dangerously close to the edge of a cliff. Through divine intervention, my wife managed to regain control and prevent our jeep from plunging down the hill. We were bewildered and unaware of how the events transpired so rapidly - we couldn't ascertain whether we had been hit, if our tires had burst or slipped, or even if there had been an earthquake. Upon exiting our jeep, we saw that the other car had sustained significant damage to the front, while our jeep had been severely crushed from behind. It became clear to us how everything had unfolded.

We were all wearing seat belts, so apart from the damage to our jeep, we were all unharmed. My wife and I initially thought that the person driving the car that hit us must have been intoxicated. With no one from the car emerging and the front end badly damaged, I approached quickly, fearing for the occupants' safety. Inside the car, an elderly couple was seated in the front, struggling to *exit as their doors were either locked or jammed due to the impact. I inquired about their well-being, and they responded that they were physically unharmed but unable to get out. I managed to open one of the doors from the outside, and with considerable effort, they were able to exit the vehicle. The elderly couple immediately apologized, expressing confusion about how the collision occurred, suggesting that they might have inadvertently accelerated instead of braking, causing the rear-end collision.*

I assured them that it was all right such accidents can happen to anyone. My wife and I offered them water and juice, then quickly called the authorities and an ambulance to ensure the elderly couple received any necessary medical attention for potential internal injuries. Once the ambulance transported the elderly couple to the hospital and our vehicles were towed to repair shops, we continued our vacation in a hired taxi. During this trip, my wife and I embraced thrilling adventures like bungee jumping, paragliding, and rafting. Internally, we felt content knowing that we chose not to escalate the situation and supported the elderly couple despite being rear-ended by them. Our positive mindset reminded us that this could have easily happened to us, and we envisioned how we would feel if someone supported us in the same way. Throughout the trip, others praised us as a radiant and happy couple, impressed by our ability to maintain positivity even after our jeep was severely damaged. Embracing forgiveness truly elevated our spirits and made our trip exceptional and unforgettable.

My wife and I realized that while we couldn't change the fact that we were hit by an elderly couple, we could control our reaction to the situation. Instead of dwelling on negativity and seeking vengeance, we chose to focus on the positive: we were safe, and no one was seriously hurt. This shift in mindset allowed us to see the event in a different light and find justification in the face of the accident. It's a reminder of the power of positivity and the impact it can have, even in challenging times.

Many successful individuals, including leaders, celebrities, and social activists, remain calm and composed despite facing numerous challenges. We can learn from their example and strive to maintain our peace of mind in the face of adversity. Building a strong social circle, fan base, and support network requires us to prioritize protecting ourselves from resentment. To be truly effective and certain in predicting and seizing our positive signals, we must practice consistently. Our *character serves as the key to shutting down our resentment and powering through with positivity. It acts as a guiding light, leading us to make the right choices and aligning ourselves with positive signals. With a solid character foundation, we can bring peace, brightness, and happiness into our lives and effortlessly tune into positive signals, shielding us from the negativity of resentment.*

When we conquer resentment, our perspective transforms, allowing us to embrace peaceful behavior and inner calm. Even in the face of provocation, our positive nature and strength of character steer us away from resentment towards a non-violent path. Adopting non-violent approaches enables us to transform destructive thoughts into constructive ones. As we master our resentment, a surge of positive energy facilitates forgiveness, a powerful force that enriches our lives and communities. True satisfaction is found in forgiveness, and as we navigate through life's myriads of situations and interactions, we must remember the immense impact of our words and actions.

In heated moments, people often say things they don't truly mean. Our actions and words during heated arguments are often fueled by negativity and don't reflect our true feelings. However, by tapping into our positive power of forgiveness, we can swiftly and profoundly transform negative situations into positive outcomes. Forgiving others, whether they wronged us intentionally or not, requires great courage, which stems from our internal positive strength. Embracing positivity and overcoming resentment allows us to genuinely forgive others.

At a college fest, I learned about a tragic incident involving a senior faculty member who lost his only son in a road rage accident. After conducting a session on the 5 natural laws with college seniors, I visited Mr. Das to offer my condolences. During our conversation, Mr. Das recounted the harrowing accident that claimed his son's life. Mr. Das, accompanied by a friend in the front seat, was driving his new SUV when a group of young men in their twenties recklessly overtook them, making provocative gestures. Feeling offended, Mr. Das and his friend accelerated their SUV, intending to assert its power. In response, the young men increased their car speed, unwittingly initiating a dangerous race. Both vehicles exceeded 100 miles per hour as they climbed a city flyover, leading to a catastrophic collision when they attempted to overtake each other. The impact caused the vehicles to overturn and collide with the flyover barricade at high speed. While Mr. Das and his friend sustained minor injuries thanks to their seatbelts and airbags, Mr. Das's son, seated in the rear without a seatbelt, suffered critical head injuries and tragically passed away in the hospital. Mr. Das now lives with profound regret, wishing he could change the decisions made that day and choosing not to engage in the reckless race. However, he understands that no amount of regret can alter the past. Let's all remember this story and vow to ignore our resentment thoughts in such situations.

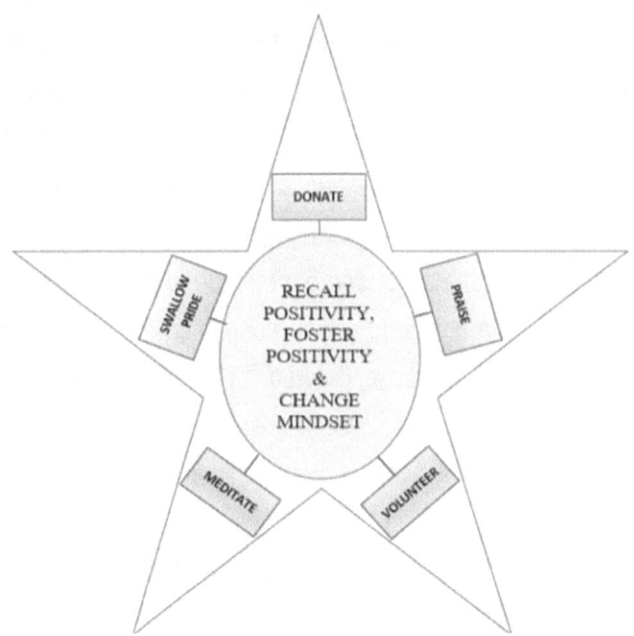

In challenging situations, embracing a positive mindset can lead us down the path of favorable outcomes. While negative thoughts may attempt to sway us, maintaining focus on positivity is crucial. It's our choice: yielding to negativity can derail our constructive journey, leading to unfavorable results in the end. To receive and embrace positive signals and thoughts, maintaining a positive attitude is crucial. A positive attitude serves as a receiver of positive signals. Engaging in activities that foster positivity is essential for cultivating such an attitude. For example, continuous exposure to online violence and violent video games can lead to an increase in violent tendencies. Similarly, constant exposure to smoking and drinking can create a desire to experiment with alcohol and cigarettes, despite being aware of their detrimental health effects. Conversely, engaging in ethical and noble pursuits can naturally shape our attitude to be positive.

It's human nature to crave recognition for our efforts. Whether it's at work, in a team, or within our families, everyone loves to feel acknowledged for their contributions. However, if we shift our focus towards uplifting and praising others, we can experience a newfound sense of freedom and contentment. To foster a culture of appreciation, we must first set aside our pride.

Embracing a more carefree attitude can be achieved by taking the initiative to recognize and commend those around us. By fostering a caring and selfless attitude, we can experience a lightness within.

Maintaining a positive outlook can help us focus on the good deeds of ourselves and others, paving the way for positivity in challenging situations. We should consider volunteering our time at organizations, places of worship, or charity events that resonate with us. This can lead to a sense of calm and humility, fostering a positive change in our attitudes. Similarly donating blood, contributing to charities, or giving old clothes to those in need can bring immense satisfaction. Maintaining a positive attitude prompts us to remember all the good things achieved by ourselves, noble individuals, or anyone else worldwide. It nurtures positivity, clears our minds, and transforms our mindset to focus on positive signals and thoughts, thereby paving the way for positivity in challenging situations. A positive attitude triggers a shift in our mindset to recognize positive signals, helping us navigate any life situation and overcome resentment.

Most of us often succumb to powerful feelings of resentment from influential sources. However, only a select few of us have the ability to handle and channel these energies with skill, turning them into opportunities. Ananya is a perfect example of this. Born into a family of doctors, she was surrounded by medical professionals— her elder brother, cousins, and relatives—all preparing for medical exams. Despite the pressure, Ananya gravitated towards a different path: law. Her parents urged her to focus on biology and start early coaching for medical exams, but Ananya found genuine happiness in studying the country's most significant legal cases and lawsuits. Ananya's heart and mind were set on becoming a lawyer. She struggled to concentrate on biology studies and instead immersed herself in stories of successful lawyers worldwide.

Ananya's cousins often made jokes and teased her about her low marks in biology. Her parents also expressed dissatisfaction and pressured her to pursue her dream of becoming a doctor. When Ananya failed to clear her medical exam, her family and relatives teased her and urged her to focus more on cracking the medical exam. Despite facing opposition and discouragement from her parents and relatives, Ananya remained steadfast in her pursuit of a career in law. Despite pressure to pursue a medical career, she remained determined to follow her passion. Her resilience paid off when she successfully cleared the law exams and gained admission to a top law college. Even after facing rejection and pushback, Ananaya remained positive and determined to prove others wrong. She focused on her goal of gaining admission to a top law institute in the country. She never wasted energy trying to convince others of her plans or future aspirations, instead choosing to listen and maintain her high level of effort. Now, practicing law in the country's supreme court, she represents clients from top industries, television actors, and high-profile individuals, all thanks to her dedication and commitment. Ananaya's parents now proudly witness their daughter's rise to success and the respect she commands.

Resentment can often feel like an obstacle in our lives, but if we learn to manage it effectively, it can become a powerful ally. Just like uncontrolled river water can cause destruction, but when channelized properly, it can be used for irrigation, drinking, and even electricity generation. Similarly, the powerful impulses of resentment when channeled with practice and care can be harnessed for positive purposes and can transform these energy packets into personal drive and motivation, steering us towards growth and success. By fostering internal peace and cultivating a strong character, we can shield ourselves from its negative effects. Maintaining a balanced perspective allows us to transform these powerful emotions into self-motivation and healthy competition, propelling us on a path of personal growth instead of dwelling on thoughts of retaliation and revenge that only serve to create obstacles in our as well as in the lives of others.

CHAPTER 3
<u>THIRD NATURAL LAW - CUPIDITY</u>

After defeating resentment, we are now preparing for our next boxing match against cupidity in the tournament. While this is as formidable as resentment, this opponent plays a crucial role in feeding stress and negativity within us. Understanding the destructive power of cupidity is essential before we enter this boxing match. This ally of the devil stress and negativity weakens our positive thinking, consumes our positive energy, and clouds our judgment, making it difficult to see the positivity and choose the right path. It gives birth to feelings of self-doubt, self-criticism, and uncertainty by creating an unfulfilling sea of desires in our minds, allowing stress and negativity to regain control over our lives. Detaching ourselves from unrealistic desires and embracing our reality is key to warding off its negative impact. By doing so, we can appreciate and enjoy what we already have.

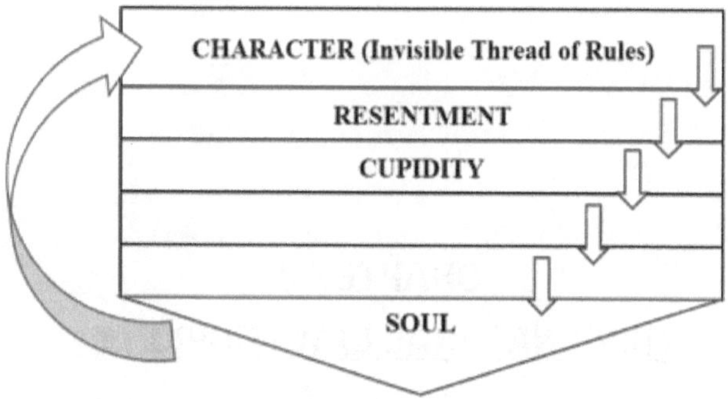

POSITIVITY SUCKER

How does cupidity create an unfulfilling sea of desires in our lives? How do stress and negativity regain and win our sturdy fort of positivity? Actually, the relentless pursuit of desires often leads to a lack of fulfillment, while stress and negativity can overshadow our optimism. Whether in business, industry, or employment, we all aspire for growth and prosperity in our endeavors. No one desires to toil in futility, with little success or profit. Our ambition is to ascend to the top and reap the rewards. To realize our aspirations and maintain a trajectory of progress, we dedicate ourselves to relentless hard work, adhering to demanding schedules, and making sacrifices along the way. Our ambition to excel and stay ahead of the competition is commendable, but it's essential to maintain a balance. We must pursue our life goals in realistic and practical ways. When we succumb to the temptation of quick gains or excessive profits, we open the door to greed and its detrimental effects. For instance, a company seeking to double its earnings overnight may resort to compromising product quality or misleading customers. While this may lead to short-term gains, it ultimately erodes trust and reputation among customers. Consider the potential consequences of a company's actions by selling subpar products or providing false information, it will damage its reputation and lose customers. On the other hand, if a company prioritizes quality and ethical business practices, it will gradually expand its reach and profit from a loyal customer base.

In our fast-paced world, we often find ourselves juggling multiple responsibilities, jobs, and businesses. Many of us believe that earning more money will lead to a better life, happiness, and stability. But we must ask ourselves: Is multitasking truly achievable? Do we have the energy and focus to excel in all our endeavors? Can wealth alone bring us inner peace and happiness? Do the rich truly lead happier lives than those in lower socioeconomic classes? It's crucial to reflect on these questions.

Our endless pursuit of wealth and power may consume us, leaving us physically and mentally drained. It's important to remember that we cannot manipulate the laws of nature for our benefit. In my social circle, I've encountered many individuals who champion multitasking as an efficient means to achieve greater results. But is multitasking truly as powerful as it's made out to be? To find out, we should put multitasking against a focused approach in a metaphorical boxing ring. During one of my corporate workshops, we conducted an experiment. We asked a group of participants to write on two separate topics for at least 300 words each within half an hour. Foreseeably, none of them could meet the word count criteria, and their writing lacked both quality and quantity due to their inability to focus on a single topic. In a subsequent session, we gave the same group a single topic to write about for 15 minutes with a minimum of 300 words. This time, most of them were able to meet the word count criteria and produced higher-quality writing. These results suggest that focusing on a single task at a time can lead to better outcomes than attempting to multitask.

Focusing on a singular approach brings both quality and quantity. In the ring of life, a focused approach always emerges victorious. It's crucial to steer clear of the distractions of pursuing multiple paths to success. Singular focus is always the winning strategy, regardless of the length of time it takes. When we attempt to juggle multiple endeavors, we often find ourselves ensnared in a web of tangled thoughts, squandering our energy and time. Only when we realize that we've expended a significant amount of our resources across numerous projects and tasks, do we seek to expedite results in order to cover our losses. Even then, we fail to recognize the error of our multitasking ways, continuing to pursue multiple objectives with various approaches and strategies, all the while neglecting the power of singular focus. It is impossible to conquer all aspects of life simultaneously, but by focusing on one at a time, we can ultimately emerge triumphant on all fronts.

The balance between our primary and secondary obligations is crucial. While we allocate time for essential routines like meals, sleep, fun, and exercise, the bulk of our day is dedicated to work or other income-generating activities. However, pursuing multiple jobs or businesses can lead to insatiable desires for more. It's a misconception to think that we can maintain all our essential routines while engaging in multiple income *streams. This multifaceted approach is more complex and time-consuming than a focused one. It's unrealistic to think we can maintain this without sacrificing something vital. It often demands sacrificing precious time with family, meals, sleep, exercise, or leisure activities, leading to a long-term negative impact on our physical and mental well-being if not managed effectively, ultimately causing stress and negativity.*

Why are we hearing so many cases of heart attacks, suicides, life-threatening diseases, divorces, drug-related deaths, etc. these days? If we look back to 15-20 years, we rarely heard or encountered such widespread negative occurrences. Nowadays, these cases are so common that it's no longer surprising to find them affecting the younger generation and people at a much younger age. Have our choices, decisions, and greed shortened our lifespan? We fall prey to stress and negativity because we are not well-prepared and do not consider the consequences of our present actions. Living in our dream world, we often fail to see the long-term effects of our choices and become short-sighted.

We must believe in the importance of growth and progress for humanity, but we must consider the limits of our desires. How much do we truly need in our lifetimes?

Is it worth sacrificing our basic needs and natural joys for excessive and extravagant lifestyles? If we choose to prioritize our careers or pursuit of wealth over our social lives, sleep, health, and relationships, we must be prepared to face the consequences of these choices in the future. The consequences of fame can negatively impact our health and distance us from our loved ones. It is a lonely journey to the top without the support of family and friends. Many public figures have suffered from the burdens of fame and ended up feeling deeply unsatisfied. We should always consider the sacrifices made for success, as nothing in this world comes for free.

Is it worth constantly pursuing wealth and material possessions, never finding contentment or peace? Perhaps we should strive for balance, understanding that true happiness and positivity comes from within, not from external sources. While money is necessary, obsessing over it is not the key to a fulfilling life. Peace and joy can be found regardless of one's financial status. It's all about focusing on positive thoughts and inner contentment. While it is possible for each of us to achieve great things in life, we must consider the cost of achieving success through excessive sacrifices. Pursuing success through unnatural or extreme means will not bring us true satisfaction, happiness, or inner peace but will ultimately suck our positivity from within. The path to success may vary for each person, but prioritizing peace, generosity, and kindness will always lead to positivity and true greatness in the end.

AFTERMATH OF GREED

The relentless pursuit of wealth and possessions can consume us, leading to a life devoid of family, relaxation, and enjoyment resulting in the loss of reputation, freedom, and even life. This insatiable cupidity can drive some to unethical and even criminal behavior, destroying their integrity and faith. We've witnessed individuals in powerful positions succumb to corruption and violence due to their unbridled avarice, resulting in imprisonment or even execution. It's a stark reminder of how the relentless pursuit of material wealth can erode our moral compass and spiritual well-being leaving us empty and disillusioned.

How do affluent parents feel when they discover that their children are failing exams, using drugs, going to jail, and have lost interest in life? Many of these parents have lamented that they rarely see their kids, even though they live under the same roof. Parents leave early in the morning to pursue their careers, while their kids sleep in after late-night parties. By the time the parents return home from work, their children are out partying again. Despite sharing a home, they have no time to connect. Is this the way to live? We need to carefully reconsider our future decisions.

We have so many examples among us where the most powerful people in the history of humankind scummed to devil cupidity. These powerful people used to rule our countries, continents, or even the entire world. Where are they all now and what happened to them? Did they live happily after conquering the world during their rule, or were they peaceful while chasing their life dreams? Many names come to mind, and their fates are known to us all. Some lost their lives during the war, some were imprisoned by their people, some were executed by the law, some faced firing squads, and some took their own lives in the end. This insatiable Cupidity cannot be tamed, not even by the most intelligent, powerful, or influential individuals in our society. Have we not learned from history or our own experiences? Our relentless pursuit of wealth and possessions only leads to stress and negativity. No number of worldly possessions can ever satisfy our desires. It's time to break free from *this cycle and seek true fulfillment beyond material wealth. We must take the time to think carefully before our lives or the lives of our loved ones slip out of our control. Postponing corrective actions may deny us the opportunity to make amends. Let's not procrastinate - let's make important decisions today and set things right now. Otherwise, we'll face the consequences of our choices and delays, which we will regret later on. Reclaiming positivity in our lives is within our grasp by making the right decisions now.*

How can we protect ourselves from the grasp of malicious cupidity? How can we lead a life of self-denial to counteract this evil? Before delving into the concept of self-preservation, let's explore an intriguing story involving a Saint and a trader. Once, a wealthy trader and his large crew were traveling from one city to another for trade. After a day of travel, the trader signaled his crew to stop near the bank of the Ganges River to rest for the night. As the crew set up their tents and prepared dinner, the trader wandered along the banks of the Ganges River. As he ventured further, he came across a young, handsome saint deep in meditation by the riverbank.

The trader saw potential in the young saint to help him sell his goods.

"Hello, dear," the trader said, showcasing his collection of gold chains and rings adorned with precious stones. "You are a healthy and handsome young man. Why don't you work for me? I am one of the most successful traders in this area."

"Why should I work for you?" the young saint asked.

"I will pay you a handsome amount of money for your work," the trader offered.

"But why do I need money?" questioned the young saint.

"With money, you can buy yourself a nice house, comfortable bed, clean clothes, gold, and many other things," the trader explained.

"But why do I need these things?" the young saint inquired.

"So that you can relax, enjoy, and be happy," the trader insisted.

The young saint replied, "I am relaxed and content here, in devotion to the almighty. Pleasure, happiness, peace, and stillness come from within, not from the outside world."

The trader fell silent, reflecting on the life lesson he had just received.

This story does not advocate abandoning everything

to become a saint, as that path is not for everyone. However, there are ways to lead a saintly life while enjoying life's comforts. This can be achieved by refining our thought processes and taking control of our daily actions and reactions. We have worked on building our character and overcoming evil resentment. Now, we have gained an understanding of cupidity and its detrimental effects. In the next few paragraphs, we will explore ways to combat and shield ourselves from this vice.

STRANGE WAYS OF LIVING

Again, the key to defeating cupidity and finding true happiness, love, peace, and joy lies within us, not in the external world. These positive emotions and feelings are inherent within us from birth. However, our relentless pursuit of material desires has obscured these innate qualities, leaving us feeling helpless and controlled by the negative forces of the modern world. By shedding the layers of endless desires, we can uncover our internal brightness and break free from the cycle of misery and pain.

We have the power to find solutions to every challenge in life. All it takes is to maintain a positive perspective and observe the world around us. Nature holds the key to *many global issues. We simply need to find a quiet place and concentrate to discover them. As human beings, we are not just physical entities, but a fusion of body, mind, and soul that represents the divine. Amidst the uncertainties and allure of this ever-changing world, we strive to mend the hardships in our lives. However, our attempts to improve or rectify things often focus on external factors. To truly enhance our lives and steer them in the right direction, we must cleanse ourselves by embarking on the inward journey within. Looking inward is the only path to end our suffering. Even with wealth and luxury, we often struggle to find inner peace. However, having material comforts doesn't guarantee happiness, just as lacking them doesn't prevent it. A person with few comforts can be happy, while someone with every amenity may be filled with sorrow. Hearing about others' difficult experiences can provide a new perspective on life.*

Let's take a moment to acknowledge those who go to bed hungry every night. It's unimaginable the suffering that both parents and children endure when they can't sleep due to hunger. Many people worldwide lack access to clean drinking water. Can we fathom living without such basic necessities? We frequently encounter stories of innocent individuals wrongly convicted and imprisoned for crimes they did not commit. Why do we postpone our happiness, tying it to material possessions and future achievements? Let's not restrict our joy to worldly objects, especially when tomorrow is uncertain.

We all know the devastating impact of war. Picture the lives of those who struggle to find food, water, or shelter during wartime. They were just like us, living normal lives until the horrors of war arrived at their doorsteps. No one can truly prepare for the upheaval of war, as it forces them to confront a whirlwind of bullets, bombs, and death in the blink of an eye. The loss of loved ones during war, whether it's a father, mother, or child, is a pain that cannot be reversed. The separation and the unimaginable sorrow they endure after losing so much in wartime is a burden we cannot fathom.

It is a universal desire for peace, and no one wishes for war. However, the harsh reality is that wars are often inevitable. The reasons for war, the methods of warfare, and the locations of conflict have changed over time. Yet, one thing remains constant - the heart-wrenching loss of loved ones. Those left behind must endure the enduring pain and sorrow. We often fail to recognize the presence of our loved ones until it's too late. Time stops for no one, and we never know when our time will come. Each day offers us the same 24 hours, and it's crucial to allocate time for ourselves, our families, and our work. In order to achieve this balance, we must abandon our old habits and embrace a new way of living. Otherwise, our plans will remain unattainable. These realities urge us to reconsider our trivial reasons for feeling discontent within the comfort of our own homes. Let's learn to appreciate what we have before longing for more.

We should get rid of strange ways of living. We need to eliminate distractions and focus on living in the present. For instance, when we're at work, we should be fully engaged in our tasks instead of daydreaming about being at home. Allowing our thoughts to wander affects our performance and can lead to negative feedback from our superiors. When we finally return home, we bring the stress from work with us, which impacts our ability to be present for our family. This can lead to misunderstandings and strain in our relationships. It's important to be mindful of our mental and emotional well-being to maintain a healthy work-life balance. Escaping our predicament involves one simple rule: "Leaving our strange way of living" Thus, we must focus on work while at the office and fully engage with our families at home.

Embrace the present! It's natural to feel envious of those enjoying lavish experiences in expensive venues. Many of us have worked hard to attain material success, but we must not compromise our values or neglect our family for the sake of material gain. In our pursuit of cupidity, we often resort to unethical means to attain wealth, power, and success. Initially, the allure of money and influence propels us into a whirlwind of fast-paced living, indulging in extravagant casinos, hotels, parties, and global travel. Life appears vibrant and exhilarating, but this euphoria is short-lived. When the law catches up with us, and we face imprisonment or even death, we are left with overwhelming regret and a desperate plea for help. However, it is too late to undo the consequences of our actions.

It is crucial to cherish our freedom, nurture meaningful relationships with family, friends, and colleagues, and uphold our values before it is too late. To live a purposeful life, we must carefully weigh the potential outcomes of our present actions. By foreseeing the implications of our choices, we can sidestep unfavorable paths. It's crucial to stay resolute in correcting our decisions to ensure that our lives carry meaning.

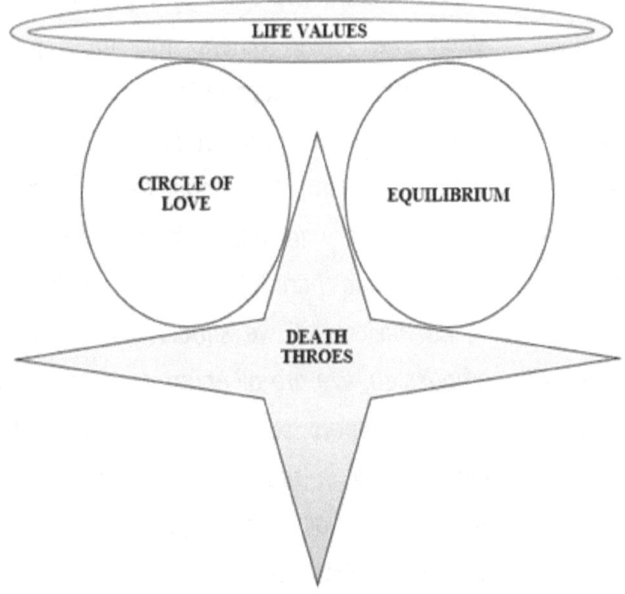

LIFE VALUES

we must prioritize kindness and avoid causing harm to others. It is crucial to extend care to all life forms, be it within our social or professional circles, within our families, or even toward our pets. Expressing goodwill toward all creatures on our planet is valuable. Demonstrating care and kindness cultivates patience and inner peace. These emotions help us resist the urge to covet what others have. A constant desire for possessions puts strain on our minds and souls. This *pressure can lead to destructive paths of depression and negativity. When we envy others for their jobs, possessions, or other achievements, our negative thoughts can drive us to act against them, leading to harmful behaviors and attempts to hinder their progress. Such negative emotions can dominate our positivity, resulting in jealousy and harmful actions. Considering how it feels to be mistreated, we should strive to treat others with compassion. We are all equal, created by the same force. Treating others poorly stems from a false belief in superiority, but in reality, we are all created equally and should respect all forms of life.*

Additionally, Dedication and commitment are other important life values. Without them, the possibility of completing any task is just a mere dream. To achieve milestones in life, these two important pillars stand tall and firm. Dedication and commitment are essential for success in both our work and personal lives. Without these qualities, life lacks meaning, and achievements become unattainable. Anyone who has reached the pinnacle of their career created memorable art, or overcome significant challenges has done so through unwavering dedication and commitment. While we can define our own set of values, certain principles, such as honesty, hard work, being true to ourselves, and never mistreating others, we must uphold in all aspects of our lives - work, goals, and family.

During my college vacation days, I used to go to the stadium for a morning walk with my school friends. It was there that I noticed Mr. Jaspal bringing his son and daughter to the stadium every morning around 4:00 am. His son would play hockey while his daughter would play badminton. Many people doubted Mr. Jaspal's children, saying that they couldn't succeed because they followed a vegetarian diet. During those days, coaches and players believed in the importance of a non-vegetarian diet for success. However, Mr. Jaspal, being a religious person, remained unfazed by the negative remarks and never let them discourage him or his children. Despite his son's requests for a non-vegetarian diet, Mr. Jaspal's unwavering beliefs and dedication never faltered. He fearlessly remained committed to fulfilling his and his children's dreams. When I started working in sales and marketing at a multinational firm, I received a proud call from a school friend informing me that a hometown boy was representing our country in the Olympics for hockey. This news filled everyone in the city, including myself, with pride. This young athlete is the son of Mr. Jaspal, and I couldn't help but recall the years of hard work that his family put in, which has finally paid off. Mr. Jaspal's unwavering belief, dedication, and commitment to nurturing his children's sporting careers are truly inspiring. Despite facing skepticism and negativity from others, he persevered, working tirelessly to fulfill his dream of providing his children with a brighter future.

In our lives, we encounter numerous situations and interact with a wide variety of people. When we strive to pursue something different, society often discourages us from investing our time and energy into new ideas. While considering various opinions is valuable for understanding potential drawbacks, it's important to disregard baseless objections. We shouldn't lend credence to individuals who criticize without knowledge or facts. If our aspirations diverge from societal norms or involve unique concepts, we should anticipate resistance. However, if we believe in our innovative ideas' positive potential and future success, we must remain resolute in our commitment and disregard the negative voices around us.

After holding on to our life values, Appreciation comes next. We should appreciate no matter how small or big our achievements. We should seek and go for our growth *in many ways but that does not mean we should forget what we already have. Dream for a fastest car is good but that doesn't mean we should dislike the car in which we drive. Dream for a big house with a huge lawn is ok, but finding no happiness inside your own home is not right. We should live every moment of life to the fullest. 'Nothing is perfect in this world', so how can we build a perfect home, own a perfect car, run a perfect business, join a perfect job, and any other worldly objects? No, it can never be possible, perfection is not in the hands of human beings or any living being in this universe.*

Perfect is the one and only one who created us, who created this nature, and who is the owner of anything to everything. We all are crafted, left to live in our own perfect world blessed by one and the only one almighty "GOD". Everyone in this world likes to be recognized and appreciated for his or her dedication, commitment, and contribution. Appreciation is a magic circle, which magically generates a tremendous amount of positive energy across our universe. We should never shy away from appreciating our parents, our life partners, our kids, our friends, our colleagues, and any lifeform for their contribution to our lives. This magical generator will never leave you alone in getting positive energy shared from the appreciation of others, you will be equally benefited by this positive energy.

CIRCLE OF LOVE AND EQUILIBRIUM

Is it possible to express 100% love to others? It seems unlikely. Love is an internal feeling that cannot be fully communicated. Demanding love in return according to specific expectations or conditions is futile. Love is powerful and its depth can only be understood by the one experiencing it. A mother expresses her love for her child in various ways, from calling them different names to singing incomplete songs. This unique bond cannot be replicated. Love is a potent tool and a precious gift to all living beings. Imagine our lives without love. it is difficult to envision thriving without it.

It's hard to imagine a fulfilling life without love. Our lives are all interconnected through a circle of love: the love for our children, their love for us, the love between siblings, friends, and families, the love for our pets, and the love for nature. This deep bond of love connects all living beings and is a precious gift. Thanks to technology, we can now experience the lives of creatures in the deepest forests and oceans from the comfort of our homes. Love is not limited to humans; it's deeply rooted in animals as well, as shown in countless videos shared online. The power of love is immense, and those truly in love are capable of making great sacrifices to prove their devotion.

Being in love is the most incredible experience, infusing our lives with meaning and purpose. When love fills our hearts, there is no room for hate or jealousy toward others. It's the key to finding fulfillment in everything we do. By loving our work, we can thrive in any environment; by loving our families, we can enrich our lives and savor every moment. Love transforms our perspective on the world and empowers us to find positivity in the face of negativity, bringing calmness and peace. Even before we meet our friends for an outing, we are filled with love and joy, eager for the journey with our closest companions. For a soldier returning home, the love they feel for their family is palpable, even before they are reunited. Love has the character of making us lose our individuality. Love forces us to follow the path which leads us back to our loved ones.

Love is a powerful force that motivates us and fills us with positivity to pursue true happiness. It's often said that everything is fair in love and war. However, some people misunderstand this aphorism as a justification for doing *anything to obtain love or win wars. It's essential to remember that those who engage in wars with ethics and moral values are ultimately the true victors. History is replete with tales of rulers who employed unethical methods to win battles, only to be remembered as villains. Conversely, those who fought with integrity, even in defeat, earned respect. Similarly, genuine love, an enduring reservoir of positivity, never condones unethical behavior. In love, it's crucial to be willing to accept defeat for the sake of our loved ones.*

When a father competes with his kids, he willingly surrenders to them. Even a defeated father finds more happiness in their love than in winning. Similarly, someone who sacrifices for the sake of their partner is the ultimate winner. Love is synonymous with cheerful sacrifice for the well-being, comfort, and even the lives of loved ones. Nowadays, obtaining things through deceit is not love. Forcing others to submit to you is not love. True love is about self-sacrifice, being willing to lose for the sake of loved ones, and being ready to sacrifice one's identity to show and feel genuine love. Winning without ethics, rules, and morality only brings negativity into our lives. We see many cases of children who, lacking love from their parents, turn to drugs, violence, and other negative behaviors. We must understand that love can never be negative, incite harm, or demand things from others. Love only teaches us to love others, bringing positivity into everyone's life.

Love is the essence of our being, and nurturing it is essential for personal growth. By tending to the seed of love within us, we can foster a life filled with positivity and joy. Love allows us to cherish each moment, whereas the absence of love or the presence of hate leads to dissatisfaction, stress, and negativity. Embracing love dispels feelings of pain, grief, and loneliness. Similar to how a rusted knife can be polished and sharpened to its former glory, we can find inner peace and fulfillment through sacrifice, ethical living, and moral values.

The marvels of the universe never fail to captivate us. We have already explored celestial bodies beyond our own, and perhaps one day, we will uncover a planet rich with life. However, the complexities of our solar system continue to elude us. Why does our solar system have only one sun? The implications of multiple suns could be catastrophic. How would we delineate day and night? How would life on Earth adapt? These questions compel us to contemplate the intricate workings of our solar system. The delicate equilibrium that sustains life on our planet is a breathtaking phenomenon. From the timing of the Big Bang to the perfect distance of Earth from the sun, the exact rotation and orbit, the composition of our atmosphere, and the interplay of natural forces, everything appears to align flawlessly to support life as we know it. Our pursuit to comprehend our existence and the conditions that foster life remains an enduring endeavor for humanity.

Maintaining balance in life is essential and unavoidable. Just envision the consequences of exercising all day, eating non-stop, binge-watching TV day and night, or not resting or sleeping at all. In each scenario, falling ill is inevitable. Our internal equilibrium must be structured so that every aspect of our plan operates in harmony, delivering the results we need. Just like a well-oiled machine, all internal parts must function smoothly in synch and produce the desired outcomes according to their design. To maintain a balanced life, it's essential to distance ourselves from unconventional lifestyles and always stay true to ourselves. Whether at work or home, giving our full commitment is crucial. Just as a balanced diet fortifies our bodies, keeping us healthy and energized, distancing ourselves from unorthodox ways of living will infuse our lives with a sense of enchantment.

The key to a fulfilling life lies in our attitude. A negative mindset and wrong motives can poison our thoughts. Chasing material possessions without balance will only lead to negative outcomes. True success and peace come from being able to sleep peacefully at night. Pursuing wealth at the expense of our health, family, and inner peace will never bring lasting satisfaction. A balanced approach, including time for health, family, work, and inner peace through activities like meditation, is essential for a meaningful life. What good is wealth if we cannot savor the pleasures of life due to poor health? Is it meaningful to earn billions but not have time to enjoy life? What is the point of building empires if we cannot find peace at night? A balanced individual who prioritizes quality time with family, good health, and appreciating the simple things in life may be more successful than someone with a big bank balance but little else.

Balance is essential in all aspects of life. Just imagine trying to work on a computer placed on a wobbly, three-legged table, or attempting to run on uneven ground. It's clear that balance makes everything smoother and more efficient. In life, balance is crucial for our eating, drinking, sleeping, and exercising habits. When we lean too much in one direction, it can lead to negativity and discomfort. Overeating leads to obesity and excessive drinking brings serious health issues. Similarly, oversleeping can result in missed opportunities and incomplete tasks. A lazy lifestyle leads to delays, frustration, and reduced productivity. It's important to maintain a balance not only in our daily habits, but also in our approach to earning and fulfilling our desires. Living a life of constant struggle for money or material possessions is not the answer. We should strive for a balanced life that allows for enjoyment, good health, and relaxation. Let's aim for a fulfilling life with our loved ones, instead of just chasing after wealth or possessions. Equilibrium a remarkable adhesive empowers us to conquer our fears of job loss, business failures, relationship breakdowns, and wavering self-confidence. A strong balance can serve as a foundation for overcoming any challenge life presents. With our understanding and clarity on equilibrium, we will not solely pursue material wealth but will also find genuine happiness and peace in our lives, and above all, it fortifies us and fosters inner tranquility.

DEATH THROES

Let's not forget the countless individuals unjustly imprisoned, the hospital patients, the homeless, and those afflicted by chronic hunger. Time is a precious commodity, but it holds a significance that goes beyond mere value. Perhaps time is a profound cosmic force that exceeds human comprehension. Even if we were to possess the entire world on our deathbed, we couldn't purchase an extra second with all our wealth. Time cannot be equated with money. While we can earn money using our time, that is just one of its smallest utilities. Time is an equal cosmic force granted to everyone on Earth. The ways in which we choose to spend our time can differ across our lives, but utilizing time solely for materialistic pursuits is futile. Consider our final moments on this planet. Life presents us with many choices. Will we truly care about money on our deathbed, when it can't even buy us a fraction of a second? Ponder upon this!

Remember this: Happiness, peace, and stillness are all found within the mind. A simple meal can bring immense joy if we are happy and content inside. Conversely, even the most luxurious or delicious food can taste bitter if we are feeling down. When we leave this *world, our material possessions such as mansions, cars, jewels, and bank accounts will all remain here. Our loved ones and everyone we've touched in our lives will continue without us. Even our own body will stay behind. So, what are we truly building in this world, and why?*

Success in life is unpredictable, whether in the entertainment industry or business. No one can guarantee a hit film, song, or winning product. However, success is not solely dependent on luck – it requires faith, commitment, and dedication. Successful individuals believe in hard work and give their best effort, leaving the outcome to fate. Focusing solely on the end result makes the journey difficult. Instead, concentrate on putting in the effort and leaving the result to nature or a higher power. This approach can help avoid negative thoughts and make the journey toward achieving life goals much smoother.

We are all destined to return to the almighty, for no one can dwell here forever. Throughout history, saints, noble minds, and revered figures have graced our world, yet none have eluded the grasp of mortality. Death is the unwavering truth of existence. Despite the efforts of tyrants, warriors, and the ruthless, none have triumphed over death, and none ever will. Material possessions are left behind and passed on for others to use. Just as we inherited from our elders, our children or the next generation will inherit from us. This is the law of nature, a reminder that we cannot take anything with us when we exit this world. There is no need to fret over accumulating wealth or to despair over lack thereof. Instead, let us live each day mindful of our ultimate moments. Our deeds are the sole currency we carry forward.

We carry with us a collection of good and bad memories and the impact of our actions, whether positive or negative. LIFE IS TO LIVE, NOT TO SPEND - as we navigate life guided by invisible natural laws of our character and rid ourselves of negative emotions, resentment, and Cupidity, we progress on our meaningful journey towards a better existence.

CHAPTER 4
<u>FOURTH NATURAL LAW - EGO</u>

In this boxing match, we face a formidable opponent: ego. Overcoming this adversary won't be easy, but it's not impossible to win. We've already strengthened our character by practicing invisible rules and defeating resentment and cupidity in the previous rounds, gaining a deep understanding of both negative and positive aspects. Now, we stand strong, ready to challenge the negative thoughts that ego brings. We are powerful and resilient! We are capable of greatness! We are unstoppable! We've made sacrifices and shown unwavering dedication. We are deserving and capable of achieving more and more.

We have all witnessed individuals who, due to succumbing to their ego have fallen from positions of power and influence. The letter "I" holds immense power, often underestimated. It's not just top leaders who are *affected by ego but 90% of the population is plagued by it. Ego has the potential to destroy positivity with a single blow, making it a formidable adversary. Its ability to change and deceive makes it even more dangerous. Once we recognize ego tricks, we can easily overcome ego influence in our daily lives.*

Constructing a dam on a river stream involves years of planning, hard work, and persistent effort. When we block the river with the dam wall, we create a manmade lake that provides us with the power of daily use of water, electricity for smart gadgets, cooking, traveling, and entertainment, enhancing our quality of life. However, if the dam wall collapses, the unleashed water can be destructive, wiping away years of hard work in a matter of seconds. In the same way that we build our character by overcoming internal struggles, we construct a barrier to prevent negativity from entering our lives. When we succeed, our body and mind become filled with positivity, which we use to create a successful and positive life for ourselves and those around us. However, when our barrier is weakened or destroyed by the powerful force of ego, negativity flows in, leaving us broken and vulnerable to our enemy's stress and negativity.

After a gap of 4 years, I again had the opportunity to

visit Dubai for work and took a day off to meet my cousin. During our chat, my cousin mentioned that Mr. Jairath, their next-door neighbor, has been unwell and there are rumors about his company filing for bankruptcy. Initially, I thought my cousin was joking, but he assured me that Mr. Jairath was struggling with his health and battling depression. It was disheartening to hear this about someone who had always been so positive. I felt compelled to visit Mr. Jairath and learn more about his situation.

I persuaded my cousin to accompany me to Mr. Jairath's place. Initially hesitant, my cousin eventually agreed after I insisted. When Mr. Jairath opened the door, I was startled by his appearance. He looked considerably older and weak, wearing a worn robe, a stark contrast to the vibrant person I had known. Despite taking a moment to recognize me, he warmly welcomed us inside. His impeccably tidy flat and his wife's warm reception made it clear that he still held himself with grace. I confronted Mr. Jairath about the rumors surrounding his company's losses, expressing my disbelief and eagerness to understand what had led to this unexpected turn of events.

Mr. Jairath initially struggled to find the right words to begin his story, but eventually, he opened up about his life's journey, success, and fall, seemingly eager to share it with someone.

In summary, he shared that he started his contracting firm as a small-time contractor with 3-4 employees. In the early days, he and his team worked tirelessly, taking on small contracting jobs day and night without weekends off. As the owner, he was also directly involved in labor work. Their big break came when a prominent builder recognized their dedication and awarded them a full-time contract after seeing their work at one of his sites. From there, they continued to achieve new heights in a short period. However, Mr. Jairath's business took a hit when he began to believe that he was the sole reason behind the company's success. An aggressive argument over a contract with one of his long-standing employees, who had been with the company since its inception, led to a disagreement. The employee expressed concerns about not being prepared to handle the project due to a low-value bid and lack of experience.

But Mr. Jairath had firmly decided to secure the contract. In addition, he resorted to using abusive language towards his old employee and even threatened to terminate his employment for interfering in his decision.

The following day, the old employee submitted his resignation. Despite this, Mr. Jairath, driven by his ego, showed no concern and proceeded with the execution of the newly obtained contract. He made substantial investments and initiated the project at full speed. However, due to the pressure and Mr. Jairath's arrogant behavior, his team eventually abandoned him mid-project. In the absence of his loyal employees and with an inexperienced team, his project was in a precarious position. Despite pouring more money into the project, his efforts were fruitless. Mr. Jairath had to leave the project site, facing substantial losses and hefty penalties from the client due to his unprofessional approach. He admitted that he should have heeded the advice of his loyal and experienced employees before taking on the contract. However, it's too late for regrets - Mr. Jairath lost everything at once and now dwells on his past. It seems like Mr. Jairath faced significant challenges due to his behavior and decision-making. It's a good reminder that maintaining professionalism and treating employees with respect is crucial for long-term success in any business. It's unfortunate that he had to learn this lesson the hard way, but hopefully, this experience will lead to better decision-making in the future.

The story teaches us that unchecked ego can be catastrophic, leading us from a path of growth and prosperity to one of depression and despair. It constantly tells us that we are always right and everyone else is wrong, eventually leaving us with nothing. Mr. Jairath lived a seemingly perfect life, starting his days with a positive approach and maintaining balance even in hectic schedules. However, he was unaware of the growing evil ego inside him, which ultimately cost him everything he had earned in his life.

Understanding the destructive nature of ego is crucial to prevent it from taking over our lives. In Hindu mythology, Ravana, despite his knowledge, succumbed to his ego and lost everything to Lord Rama. Even in today's families, we struggle to find peace and maintain healthy relationships. The root of this issue lies within us, as ego affects everyone, causing conflicts and hindering growth. It's time to recognize and address the destructive power of ego in our lives. We struggle to find peace and happiness with a family. Why can't we maintain healthy relationships with our parents, spouse, or kids? Why don't we have time to listen to our parent's concerns, or why don't our parents want to listen to their kids' concerns? We need to understand that the problem of this evil ego does not lie outside, it is rapidly growing inside all of us. This ego is growing and controlling almost everyone on our planet.

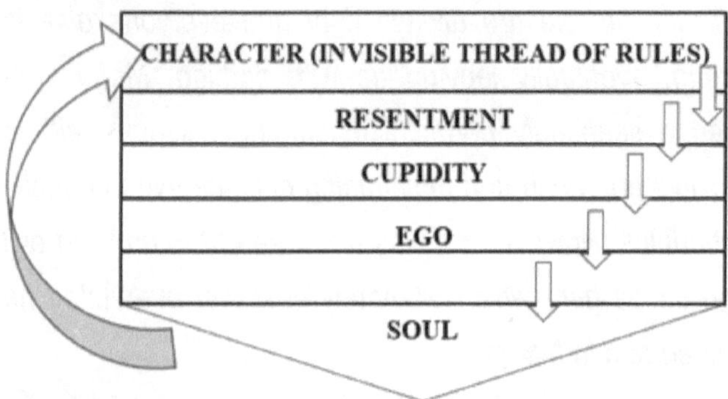

I recently had a conversation with a startup owner in my hometown who expressed frustration about the difficulty of finding dedicated and honest employees. She believes that the high turnover rate is impacting her business and is seeking solutions. I suggested observing her employee's behavior at the office to better understand the situation. After attending various meetings and gathering feedback from employees, I presented her with a candid assessment of her startup and proposed an improvement plan.

BRUTAL FACTS:

(1) No medical insurance scheme for employees

(2) No one celebrates birthdays or anniversaries in the

office.

(3)　No pick-and-drop service for employees in the morning or who work late hours.

(4)　Leverage senior employees to come a bit late to the office.

(5)　Low involvement of new employees in future target settings.

(6)As owner, she never involved herself with junior teams. She mostly reviews and discusses with top management only.

ROAD TO RECOVERY:

(1) Corporate Medical Insurance Scheme for all employees.

(2) Birthdays, anniversaries, or other achievements should be celebrated inside the office to increase personal touch.

(3) Start of pick and drop service at least for late hours of the day, may start with female employees initially as a pilot run.

(4) All employees should come and leave the office at the same time.

(5) Involvement and discussion with junior-level employees in future decisions that will affect them in the future.

(6) As the owner of the company, it's essential for her to be involved at the grassroots level of her organization. This doesn't necessarily mean she has to attend every official meeting full-time. However, making an effort to attend even the first 10-15 minutes at the beginning or the last few minutes of meetings can make a significant difference. The involvement of the company owner at that level can instill confidence and provide a boost to both new and seasoned employees.

She acknowledged the existing gaps and areas for improvement but expressed her reluctance to participate in junior-level meetings. As the owner and top executive of the company, she feels that attending such meetings would be inappropriate. She believes that if she were to sit with junior-level employees, it would undermine her position as the owner and leader of her venture. Her ego as the company owner is a significant factor, as she is unwilling to engage with junior-level employees. However, this attitude has resulted in her being disconnected from the real challenges and concerns at the grassroots level of her organization, contributing to a low employee retention rate in her startup.

MEGA-BOMB EXPLOSION

Is it ever possible to live without ego? Do selfless deeds truly exist? Can we find individuals who have conquered their egos? What are the strategies and ways for overcoming ego? Ego can manifest in various forms, and it is often accompanied by its allies, resentment, and cupidity. Overcoming ego requires addressing these allies, which may be easier since they have been defeated and knocked out by us before, but ego always shields them from defeat.

When we believe that we are the best, that no one is better than us, and that we know everything, our ego is at play. This ego prevents us from embracing a positive mindset that encourages us to listen to others, continuously learn, and then share our knowledge. Ego stops us from listening to other perspectives, instead insisting that we always command, never yield, and are right. It convinces us that others are ignorant and that we should not pay attention to them. When our egos take over, we often lose our positivity and resort to yelling, shouting, and fits of rage, which invites resentment. Our minds then push us to seek immediate control, wanting everything at once, from high profitability overnight to doubling our income in an instant, which sends an invitation to cupidity. When these impulses hit us, we feel no choice but to dance to their tune and become their prey.

Even when we have successfully overcome our adversaries and built a strong fortress to shield ourselves from these malevolent forces of stress and negativity, they still manage to strike us down. Our resilient dam wall crumbled under the force of a mega-bomb ego, unleashing a flood of negativity into our lives. In these moments, we feel deeply wounded and betrayed by the world around us. Despite our best efforts, everything seems to veer off course, leaving us feeling vulnerable and powerless and it's easy to believe that this is simply the way things are meant to be.

When stress and negativity once again seep into our beings, we find ourselves in a state of misery, feeling deceived, forsaken, and neglected. In response, we take steps back into the negative realms of smoking, drugs, alcohol, gambling, and ignoring loved ones in search of solace.

Why did our positivity fail to protect us? Why did our strong fort of positivity not save us? Why did our positive strategy prove ineffective in the face of the mega bomb ego? Let's understand why our solid system failed.

Imagine squeezing a person's neck when they are trying to sing in a competition. They would never be able to complete their song, no matter how talented or prepared they are. Similarly, can a plant survive if covered completely under a pile of dry grass? All our efforts will be wasted, and we can never reap the fruit.

But if we remove the pile of grass and take care of our plant, slowly, it will give us fruit. Same way think about trying to drink juice or water from a bottle with a cap on. You can't satisfy your thirst without opening the bottle first. Similarly, no matter how much positivity we have inside us, our ego can bury it under a pile of grass. We need to remove that barrier to unleash our full potential.

The smoldering embers of our actions don't ignite instantly. They slowly kindle when we stray from our guiding principles. Life often thrusts us into situations where we feel compelled to abandon our moral compass. We may believe that deviating from our values just once won't amount to much, but even a small breach can eventually lead to a catastrophic collapse. A small breach in a dam wall can lead to catastrophe. Similarly, we must not overlook or underestimate the importance of our values. They should be upheld with utmost care and consideration. It is crucial to periodically reassess our guiding principles. However, in many cases, we succumb to rage, spiraling into a dark abyss of vices, engaging in conflicts with loved ones, and setting unattainable goals. We continue to plummet until we are ensnared in our egos. When we sense our equilibrium slipping, when resentment and cupidity threaten to overpower us, or when we find ourselves succumbing to temptation, we must return to our invisible thread of core values and

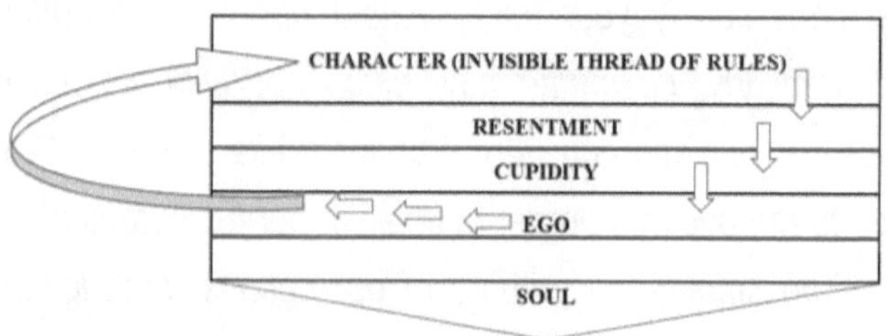

Instead of succumbing to stress and negativity, brought on by inflated egos and the pitfalls of life, we should strive to reinvent and reexamine our character. Rather than resigning ourselves to a life of failure, we must muster the strength to fight back and rebuild our character, steering clear of drugs, alcohol, or smoking.

Revisiting our core values and principles will provide the clarity that may have been obscured by the glare of *success or a prolonged disconnect from our true selves. Think of when we first learned to drive a car. Initially, we were completely focused on the road – not allowing anyone else in the car to distract us – concentrating solely on the accelerator, brake, and clutch. However, as we gained experience, we began to look around, engage in conversations, and even listen to music while driving, with our actions becoming second nature through practice. Similarly, revisiting our character and principles won't require much time, as we have already grasped them once before. This time, we simply need to revise, and our derailed lives will naturally find their way back on track.*

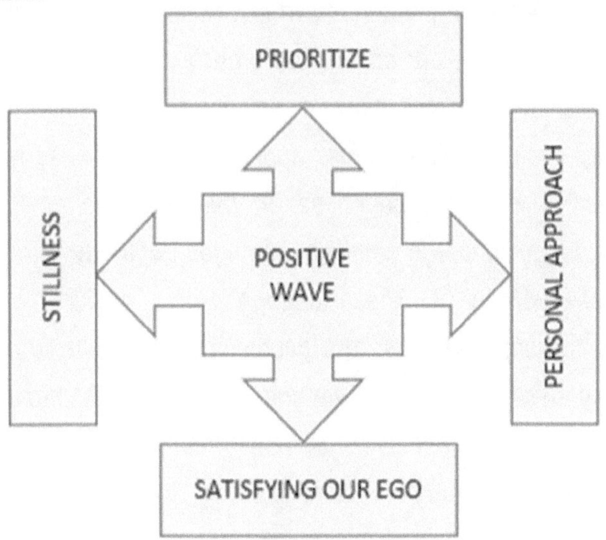

CREATING A FOUR DIRECTIONAL POSITIVE WAVE

When driving at 150 mph on a straight highway, attempting to take a turn without slowing down can lead to losing control of the car. Similarly, the impact of ego in our fast-paced lives can lead to unexpected crashes and upheavals. To navigate through life's twists and turns, it is crucial to recognize the importance of knowing our ego and learn to apply brakes and pauses when necessary.

We must recognize this crucial principle of life: every day is unique and distinct from the last. Even if we follow the same routine, our experiences and perspectives evolve with each passing day.

While we may not perceive significant changes within ourselves daily, our continuous growth and development shape our perceptions and emotions. Embracing this daily evolution allows us to appreciate the richness and diversity of our experiences. In the grand scheme of nature, we undergo countless changes each day without even realizing it. These changes, both physical and mental, shape who we are becoming. By prioritizing our daily tasks and planning, we gain valuable insight into our progress and direction. Without this focus, we risk wandering without purpose or direction.

PRIORITIZE AND PERSONAL APPROACH

Focusing on priorities brings peace of mind. For instance, when faced with 10 tasks, choosing the top 5 based on their importance in terms of profitability, relationships, or other significant factors allows for a balanced approach to the day. Completing these top tasks brings a sense of fulfillment and contentment, knowing that realistic goals have been accomplished as planned. Halfway through our tasks, we find contentment and peace.

Unfinished work no longer weighs on us. Prioritizing our tasks brings satisfaction and confidence, allowing us to follow a clear and structured path. Rather than attempting to tackle everything at once, we should focus on prioritizing our tasks and planning to avoid unnecessary pressure on us.

If my cousin's neighbor from Dubai had taken a more personal approach with his employees, he could have prevented the downfall of his team. By understanding that the project was not suitable for his company, he could have directed his efforts elsewhere, leading to greater success. Unfortunately, his ego led him to believe that he was the smartest person in the company, causing him to lose sight of the character that had initially propelled his success. His outburst of resentment towards a loyal employee and the allure of false profits due to cupidity ultimately led to the demise of his once-successful empire in Dubai. It's clear that prioritizing a personal approach over ego-driven decisions is crucial for sustained success and a positive wave.

The power of a personal approach is the key to overcoming ego and connecting with positivity. A personal approach involves understanding and empathizing with the thoughts, feelings, and perspectives of others. It's about making a genuine impact by complement, motivating, inspiring, influencing, and encouraging others on a personal level.

This approach is not about external rewards or benefits, but about creating meaningful connections and fostering personal growth.

During a trip to Uttarakhand, my friends and I booked a cab for a week with a driver from the same hometown as our destination. The driver kindly offered to stay at his home overnight if we preferred not to travel after dark, and we happily agreed. His considerate gesture was reflected in his driving and attitude, making our journey enjoyable and relaxed. Upon our return, we gave the travel agency a five-star rating to express our satisfaction with the entire experience.

When we planned our outing for next year, we once again reached out to the same travel agent to arrange a cab for all of us. Unfortunately, the cab driver assigned to us was not polite and drove recklessly. Despite our repeated requests to drive safely, the driver continued to display dangerous behavior. Despite the unpleasant experience with the driver, our trip to the hills was amazing.

However, we felt compelled to give a one-star rating to express our dissatisfaction with the travel agency. Following this, I received a call from the travel agency supervisor, who asked me to share our negative experience and the reason for the low rating.

After recounting the entire unfortunate experience, the supervisor explained that the driver had to cancel his leave to accommodate our booking, as no other drivers were available at the travel agency. This may have contributed to the driver's unprofessional behavior. To make amends for our bad experience, the supervisor offered us a 50% discount on our next booking and assured us that such incidents would not occur in the future.

It's important to remember that combining our priorities with a personal approach can lead to highly positive results. This blend helps us set aside our egos daily. The key rule of a personal approach is to strive for a positive outcome, which can never be a negative result.

When we achieve success through hard work and dedication, it is natural to feel proud and enjoy the rewards. Sharing our accomplishments with our loved ones is important, but it's crucial to stay mindful of the fine line between pride and ego. Embracing our achievements and aspirations is healthy, and we should strive to lead a fulfilling and abundant life. There's nothing wrong with aiming for the very best and living life to the fullest.

When we achieve success and start enjoying the fruits of our labor, it's natural to feel a sense of pride. However, it's important to ensure that our pride doesn't turn into arrogance. We must avoid thinking that no one else deserves the same benefits or success as us. True pride comes from humility and the willingness to see others succeed as well.

Mr. Kunal, the owner of a swimming academy, once shared an inspiring story about one of his talented swimmers. Among the many promising athletes he has trained, this particular student's achievements left a lasting impact. Vishal, a gifted swimmer, has consistently brought home gold medals from both private and state-level competitions. Mr. Kunal had high hopes for Vishal's potential inclusion in the national team and believed that his exceptional speed and technique would one day secure a gold medal for the country in international competitions. Vishal's reputation and potential were well-known in the academy and the city.

Despite his dedication to the sport, Vishal began to exhibit signs of ego, preferring to practice alone and distancing himself from other swimmers. Recognizing Vishal's commitment, Mr. Kunal provided him with the space and focus he needed by allowing him to train separately.

One day, Vishal arrived early for his swimming practice and entered the pool, asking other swimmers to leave. While some swimmers complied, others insisted it was their scheduled time and refused to vacate the pool. In the ensuing confrontation, Vishal's ego led to harsh words and eventually a physical altercation.

Despite initially overpowering his opponent, Vishal slipped on the wet tiles and suffered a severe head injury. Rushed to the hospital, he survived, but with memory loss. This tragic story serves as a powerful lesson, illustrating the destructive potential of unchecked ego. Mr. Kunal often cites Vishal's story to remind his players to celebrate their achievements without succumbing to arrogance. He urges them to embrace humility and support their peers, ensuring that pride never transforms into a toxic ego.

SATISFYING OUR EGO

It is important to acknowledge that our ego should not always be disregarded. If our ego presents a minor obstacle to achieving something great, it is worth addressing. However, we must approach ego satisfaction with caution, as an inflated ego can lead to negative outcomes. Determining whether our ego is minor or has no impact on the overall strategy is crucial in deciding whether to pursue ego satisfaction.

My wife and I wanted our daughter to learn how to swim. We enrolled her in a nearby swimming coaching center. She adores swimming pools, and once she's in the water, she never wants to leave. However, when it comes to learning from the coach, she becomes the most stubborn member of her group. She comes up with all sorts of reasons such as stomach aches, water temperature being too cold or too warm, cleanliness concerns, headaches, arm pain, or leg pain.

All the other kids had surged ahead in their swimming skills, but my daughter had been hesitant to join in for a whole week. My wife and I assumed she had lost interest in swimming, so we decided to let it go. But seeing her have so much fun in the pool, I couldn't shake the feeling that something wasn't right. She seemed to enjoy the water more than anyone else in her group, so why wasn't she taking lessons from the coach? We tried to encourage her to learn to swim in every way we could, but we never succeeded. Eventually, we lost hope and stopped trying to motivate her. After a while, she even stopped going to the swimming pool.

One afternoon, I treated my daughter to her favorite pizza and encouraged her to share more about her swimming experience. Initially hesitant, she eventually confided that her dislike for her swimming costume had been holding her back. It turns out, the color of the costume was the culprit.

Realizing this, I took her to choose her own costume, and within just 15 days, she was confidently swimming with her peers. This experience taught me that personalized attention and addressing individual preferences are crucial for success. This goes to show *that ego can manifest in various ways, but the key to success lies in a combination.*

STILLNESS

Adopting a prioritized way of working can bring about a positive change in our lives. Without a clear direction, it's difficult to make progress. By prioritizing our daily, weekly, or monthly tasks, we can achieve better results and invite positivity into our lives. If we examine the lives of influential figures, we can observe that their unwavering focus on personal approach played a significant role in their success.

These remarkable individuals didn't do everything, but they upheld their character, empathized with others, and maintained an exceptional personal approach, which contributed to their greatness. It's important to remember that when these elements come together, the outcome is always a positive wave in the ocean of positivity, never negative. By integrating these principles, we can effectively diminish our ego and its negative impact.

Once we overcome our ego, we can experience the gift of stillness. Inner stillness is truly rewarding and unattainable as long as the ego holds sway. It is achieved by those who are genuinely at peace within themselves, free from the grip of ego. Inner stillness offers numerous benefits. Just like how we can't see our reflection in the rushing waters of a river, a mind caught up in wandering thoughts prevents us from finding peace. Stillness allows for reflection and clarity, providing peace and satisfaction. This stillness enables us to see things clearly, just like a calm river in which we can see our reflection.

However, a mind at ease can provide clarity and contentment, allowing us to see things for what they truly are. Someone who cultivates inner stillness experiences greater happiness and peace, content with whatever they have. In contrast, ego-driven individuals incessantly pursue more, leading to dissatisfaction and negativity. We often covet what others possess, believing it would bring us greater happiness. However, by embracing inner stillness, we can find contentment and joy in our own possessions, no matter how modest. A serene mind radiates positivity, enriching our lives and those around us.

A few years ago, I began experiencing knee pain due to my long hours of driving. Upon consulting with one of my family doctors, I was advised to incorporate cycling into my exercise routine. Before this, I had never considered purchasing a bike for myself. However, as I *explored the bicycle market, I found it intriguing and ended up buying a mountain bike (MTB). Following my doctor's recommendation, I started cycling to alleviate my knee pain. Being an outgoing individual, I tend to readily make new friends. I am open and approachable, often initiating conversations and showing a genuine interest in others. Cycling quickly became an integral part of my life, and I found it to be a captivating and essential activity.*

During my cycling days, I had the privilege of meeting an 80-year-old Army Colonel who dedicatedly rode his MTB to the mountains every day. His unwavering determination and passion captivated everyone in the MTB community. Not only was he a professional MTB rider, but he also had a knack for humor, often entertaining the group with his jokes during breaks. Rain or shine, hot or cold, the Colonel never missed a day of cycling, always arriving at the starting point ahead of everyone else.

His profound expertise in cycling and techniques made him the natural leader of the MTB gang, and despite being 50-60 years older than the others, he effortlessly kept pace with the younger cyclists.

One morning, the Colonel didn't show up for our cycling session. Concerned, I called him but received no answer. We went cycling without him, reminiscing about the moments we had with Colonel and the lessons he taught us. The next morning, he was absent again, and I decided to visit his house if he didn't show up the following day. When he finally returned, everyone was relieved and happy to see him. Despite our questions about his absence, Colonel remained lighthearted and didn't give a serious answer.

In the past two days, we all recognized the colonel as the heart and soul of the MTB gang. Ever since then, we've been cycling alongside the colonel every day. One morning, a young cyclist asked the colonel about his exact age, to which the colonel replied straightforwardly and seriously that he is 20 years old. Although everyone laughed, the persistent young cyclist asked the colonel once more about his exact age. The colonel humorously explained that since his birthday is on February 29th and only comes around once every four years, he counts 1 year for every 4 years, making him 20 years old. However you choose to calculate it, for him, he is 20 years old, and in the next 4 years, he will be a year older. His response showcased genuine positivity and humor.

One evening, I had the chance to meet a colonel at my uncle's dinner party. It was a surprise to discover the *connection between my uncle and the colonel. I was used to seeing the colonel only in the mornings. His demeanor and attitude among his peers were truly admirable, as he lived life to the fullest. After everyone left, my uncle and I discussed the colonel's kind-hearted nature and grand lifestyle.*

My uncle revealed that the colonel had recently lost his wife and had no children. Despite being alone in the world, it was his courage, positivity, and values that kept him going. I was shocked to learn that he cycled with us every morning, and none of us knew about the tragic event in his life. Upon reflecting, I realized that he had missed cycling for two days around the time of his wife's passing. However, when he returned, he showed the same courageous, strong, and larger-than-life attitude.

The next morning, upon seeing the colonel again, I felt compelled to offer my condolences. Upon hearing the news of his wife's passing, the entire MTB gang was taken aback and rallied around the colonel in support.

I questioned why the colonel had not shared this information sooner. He responded by explaining that death is inevitable, and rather than dwelling on it, we should focus on making the most of our time. This profound truth inspired me to shift my perspective and prioritize living to the fullest until our time is up.

The tranquility and serenity that accompanies stillness offer us a fresh perspective on life. It reminds us that we have no control over life outcomes or how the future unfolds, so there's no need to fret about it. Every one of us has an expiration date in this world, and when our time comes, we will depart for the next realm. What we carry with us after death are our attitudes and the memories of how we lived our lives.

CHAPTER 5
FIFTH NATURAL LAW - TUNNELS OF WISDOM

One evening, a young boy accompanied by his father visited a bustling circus. The boy reveled in the vibrant lights, indulged in his favorite vanilla chocolate ice cream, and enjoyed various games and rides. His joy was palpable as he temporarily escaped his life's challenges. However, amidst the crowd leaving the circus, the boy became separated from his father. Despite calling out and searching in his wheelchair, the once joyful surroundings now only served as a painful reminder of his current predicament. Without warning, his father swept in and enveloped him in a tight embrace. Overcome with emotion, the child clung to his father, finally realizing that the true source of his happiness and joy was not the shops or the taste of his favorite ice cream, but the comforting presence of his father.

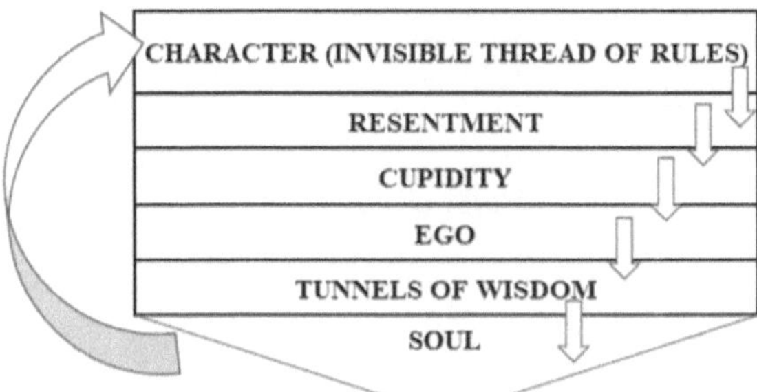

We have established a solid foundation of character by adhering to invisible rules and core values. By overcoming resentment, cupidity, and ego

In this final stage of our journey, we will traverse the tunnels of wisdom to discover ancient, timeless wisdom that will fortify our inner faith and enable us to embrace positivity. These sacred tunnels hold the key to lasting happiness and peace, providing the energy we need to vanquish negativity. As we enter these tunnels, we no longer battle alone. We gain a new life coach, an ally of positivity, to support us in all our endeavors. Navigating these tunnels of wisdom will offer guidance and enlightenment, ensuring we stay on the path to connect with our soul—the ultimate source of positive energy. To hear the heavenly voices within the tunnels, we must earnestly practice and implement these 5 natural laws in our lives.

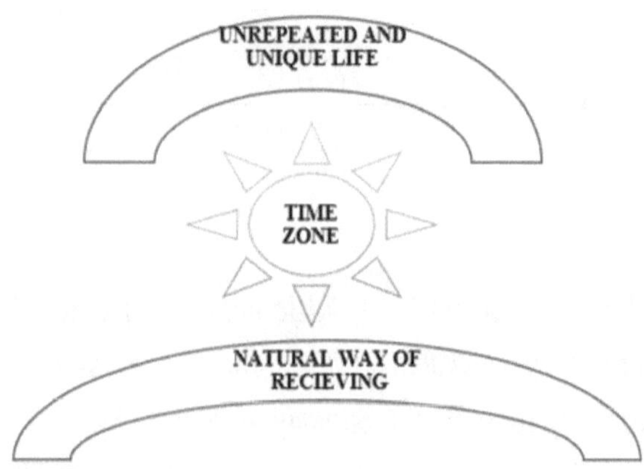

UNREPEATED AND UNIQUE LIFE

Change is inevitably the only constant, as time is continuously evolving. Organizations and individuals may follow the same principles, values, and procedures, yet encounter different challenges and situations daily. This leads us to question whether everything is influenced by time alone or if there are additional factors at play.

The enigma of life on our planet prompts us to question its supposed perfection and the unpredictability of its outcomes. Despite being a suitable place for life, our planet's imperfections raise doubts about the true nature *of its suitability for life. The analogy of planting seeds under seemingly identical conditions and yet experiencing different outcomes compels us to contemplate the underlying mysteries of life that may transcend human understanding. It is evident that technological advancements have failed to unravel these inner mysteries, as exemplified by the unpredictable nature of birth and death.*

Living a life isolated on a hilltop, surrounded by luxury but devoid of human connection, is a stark existence. Our relentless pursuit of success and material wealth often leads us astray from life's true essence. Without the joy of sharing our lives with loved ones, our accomplishments lose their meaning. Such a solitary life is akin to being a lone tree in a vast jungle or a solitary stone in the desert. In today's digital age, we are bombarded with an overwhelming number of choices and information. Whether it's deciding on which brand to buy from countless options, the decision-making process can be daunting. With so many options available, it's important to make informed and confident decisions, it's important to carefully consider what to buy and why not to buy in today's time. We are faced with an overwhelming array of choices, leading to confusion when making decisions.

Rather than thoroughly researching and evaluating options, we often rely on the opinions and feedback of others.

While this may be efficient for selecting everyday products, it raises the question of whether we should apply the same approach to major life decisions such as career moves, relationships, education, and investments. These significant choices, which profoundly impact our lives, are typically influenced by the advice of friends, family, and peers. When a big decision in our lives turns out well, everyone rushes in to celebrate and take credit for our success. But if things go wrong, suddenly no one wants to take responsibility and starts blaming us for the failure. To achieve success, we must take control of our decisions, while also carefully considering the opinions of others. Their perspectives can provide valuable insights and help us see both the positive and negative aspects of our situations.

Just as we each have our unique way of making tea with various ingredients, everyone has their preferences and choices. Just like how we don't like every combination of tea, it's okay for people to have different preferences. Discriminating against someone based on their tea blend choice is simply wrong. We are all unique in our ways, just like the colors of a rainbow. It's impossible to live someone else's life entirely. Our children have their perspectives, and spouses react differently to life's challenges. No living being on our planet can be 100% identical. When a group of people facing the same situation will respond in unique ways, each of us lives in our time zone, and no two individuals are completely alike in character, nature, appearance, behavior, thoughts, or emotions. This idea applies not only to humans but also to corals, insects, animals, birds, fish, reptiles, mammals, and plants. It's important to acknowledge that each of us is unique, with different strengths, weaknesses, and perspectives.

The message is powerful and resonates deeply with the importance of accepting and celebrating the uniqueness of individuals. It emphasizes the negative impact of trying to impose our thoughts and expectations on others and instead encourages embracing diversity and individuality. The analogy of sowing the bad seed of stress and negativity is vivid and thought-provoking. The reminder that every individual is unique and possesses special qualities is a valuable perspective to keep in mind. This message serves as an important reminder to appreciate the variety of experiences and perspectives that exist in the world. By respecting and considering other people's viewpoints, we can avoid imposing our beliefs on them. It's unnatural to expect everyone to agree with us all the time, and this mindset can lead us away from our true path toward unlocking our ocean of positive power, the soul.

NATURAL WAY OF RECEIVING

To truly comprehend the nature of success and failure, we must acknowledge that we have little control over the outcomes. Nature holds all the power, and we cannot influence it in any way. So what can we do? Should we simply wait for our fate to unfold? Consider this: can we predict the size of a banyan tree from its seed? Of course not. However, by nurturing the seed with water, manure, and protection from harsh weather, we can witness its transformation into a magnificent tree. Similarly, we must dedicate ourselves to our goals with hard work, sincerity, passion, and commitment. Success requires honest and consistent effort. Yet, it's important to recognize that not everyone will attain their aspirations through these means.

Just imagine the impact if everyone obtained everything they desired. It would lead to chaos on our planet, wouldn't it? Each one of us has different desires and aspirations, but what if all these conflicting wishes were granted simultaneously? Picture a world where someone's dream of having a grand mansion is fulfilled, while another person's wish to destroy such a mansion and the lives within it also come true. Imagine someone striving to rule a country and another seeking to bring it to ruin. Similarly, one individual endeavors to build a successful business, while another seeks to destroy their own. If all these desires were to be fulfilled at once, our world would descend into chaos. It is crucial to aspire to achievable goals that contribute positively to our world. Positive desires and wishes attract natural forces to aid in their realization.

We have all experienced instances where tasks are effortlessly completed and encounters with helpful individuals lead to timely successes. This is the result of the flow of positive energy within us, influencing those around us to act in ways that align with our goals. One of my friends, Johnny was a dedicated socialist, tirelessly helping those in need in his community. He was an active member of the Red Cross Society and other NGOs in the area. His lifelong passion for paragliding drove him to become a professional paraglider. During a competition in *the Himalayan ranges, he lost control of his paraglide due to high-speed winds and sudden weather changes. He veered off course and crashed in an unknown valley, sustaining injuries from the dense forest and the impact of the ground. While his crewmates and colleagues feared the worst, they could only watch helplessly, hoping for the best in this dire situation.*

At the same time, an ambulance swiftly transported a biker with a broken leg to the city hospital. Upon seeing Johnny crashing into the woods, the biker with a broken leg insisted ambulance driver and helper bring Johnny to the hospital along with him. Fortunately, Johnny's crash site was close by, and the ambulance team quickly reached him and brought him on board. Despite being unconscious and seriously injured, Johnny's life was saved after undergoing surgeries at the city hospital. Despite the harrowing experience, Johnny remains unwavering in his pursuit of becoming a paragliding world champion. He considers himself incredibly fortunate to have been promptly assisted by the ambulance team.

The timely arrival of the ambulance coincided with Johnny's crash, and it was the biker who witnessed him being brought out on a stretcher. It's incredible how Johnny's determination to pursue his life dreams persisted even after the accident, and we believe that it's his profound dedication to helping others that played a part in his miraculous survival. Perhaps it was the combination of fate and nature that intervened in his favor.We are all familiar with the numerous stories of people who found themselves helpless during accidents, often paying a heavy price, or even losing their lives. Nature wields immense power, while we are mere specks in the universe. It's crucial to align our thoughts and energy in harmony with nature. Our lives should be dedicated to giving back to nature, not just taking. Together with nature's forces, we can achieve the unimaginable. However, if nature turns against us, we risk losing our very identity.

To improve our lives, we must align ourselves with the natural laws that bring positivity to our lives and the lives of others around us. Instead of expecting others to change for us, we should take the initiative and embody the positive change we wish to see. We should strive to be a part of the natural life chain by taking care of our environment, our planet, and the animals and their habitats. Do we truly believe that our mother earth is more beautiful with only the human race and no other living beings? Our planet is the home for all living beings, and as the highest order on earth, it is our responsibility to take care of our home and the beings below us in the food chain. Nature has provided us with everything we need to live a happy and fulfilling life, but our negative desires for power, control, and excess can lead to destruction and chaos.

At times, we encounter situations where progress seems to come to a standstill. Despite our best efforts and hard work, obstacles prevent us from moving forward. It can be frustrating to witness others receiving assistance while we are left behind, especially when someone obstructs our path and hinders our progress. It's natural to wonder how different circumstances could have led to a more favorable outcome. We must realize that nature has the power to take everything away from us in an instant. History has shown us how dictators who sought control and spread hate ultimately lost everything when nature turned against them. We must respect and nurture the delicate balance of nature to thrive and coexist harmoniously. We must align our goals and desires with nature and then exert our sincere efforts to achieve them. If it's not meant for us, no force in the universe can make it happen. We shouldn't be disheartened if the results don't align with our plans.

Always strive for the best and leave the rest to nature. We must acknowledge the fact that we are part of the natural order and should accept every outcome with humility and gratitude.

Let's confront stress and negativity head-on with the force of the Trueman ship. We must confront and acknowledge all realities, whether they are right or wrong. Developing our character is essential, and we must continually combat the demons of resentment, cupidity, and ego whenever they attempt to re-enter our lives. Just as we become skilled through practice, the same applies to these 5 natural laws. With continuous practice, we can all become experts in each law. Eventually, these 5 natural laws will become deeply ingrained in us, becoming inseparable parts of our internal system. Even if we are acting consciously, our subconscious mind will align itself to protect us from stress and negativity.

Have you ever seen a lion trying to eat grass? No matter how hungry, weak, or injured the lion may be, it will never eat grass. Similarly, have you ever witnessed an elephant hunting for meat to satisfy its hunger? Nature has designed herbivores and carnivores in distinct ways. Similarly, as we develop our inner strength through the practice of these 5 natural laws and begin to see results, we must proceed with caution and attentiveness. Because just like choosing a mode of travel from London to Paris, there are various ways to achieve our goals. However, there is always the fastest way. Once we find the fastest way, we can use the extra time to indulge in shopping, explore the city, relax, or go sightseeing. Achieving our ultimate life goals, whether it's owning a billion-dollar company, becoming the fastest car racer, or gaining a billion subscribers on a channel, requires efficient and effective strategies in the right place and at the right time. Consider this: is it more fulfilling to realize our dream of becoming a professional bodybuilder at the age of 20, or to achieve that level of fitness and physique at the age of 45? If we aspire to become a professional bodybuilder during high school, it's essential to pursue and accomplish that dream as quickly as possible at the right time only.

To achieve our dreams and goals, it's crucial to follow the right path with caution and attentiveness. Regularly checking and rechecking our progress is vital to avoid veering off course. These quick reassessments are guided by 5 natural laws that help us stay on track. Just as we review our answers during exams to ensure top performance, this ongoing diligence is essential for *reaching our ambitions swiftly and effectively.*

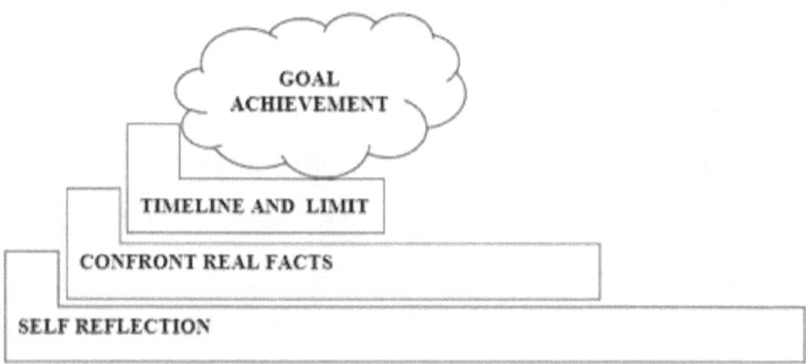

GOAL ACHIEVEMENT

In the final round of this boxing match, success hinges on self-reflection, facing the facts, and establishing clear timelines and boundaries. When setting goals, it's essential to devise a practical and achievable strategy. Unrealistic plans are bound to fail. As we pursue our objectives, maintaining the right pace and staying on course are crucial. Regular self-assessment is the first step in effectively validating our progress and ensuring we are following the right path. Nothing is impossible in this world. With proper planning and effective working, everything is achievable. Self-reflection is a crucial tool that assesses our self-competence to be in the driver's seat. Continuous improvement during our journey is essential to avoid mistakes and bridge gaps. If additional training or courses are necessary for our goals, we must promptly identify these needs to avoid falling behind schedule.

Confronting real facts is vital in fortifying our strategy and achieving our goals. To achieve business success and growth, it is imperative to have a deep understanding of each step in the complete business cycle. Expertise or knowledge in every aspect of the business is crucial. When expertise is lacking, it is essential to bring in specialists who can manage different segments of the business. Timely recruitment of experts is crucial for business growth and sustainability. It is a misconception to believe that the business can run smoothly without experts, as this can lead to the downfall of the business. Even with a complete team of experts, ongoing training and skill enhancement are necessary to identify and address the needs of the business processes. Monitoring the competition and understanding market dynamics are equally important. By facing reality and not being oblivious to the competitive landscape, businesses can better position themselves for success.

Dreaming is akin to being enthralled by a movie in a theatre. Just like in a comedy scene, we experience genuine joy, momentarily forgetting our real-life concerns.

Similarly, during poignant moments, we may feel genuine sadness and shed tears, blurring the line between fiction and reality. When faced with a horror scene, the fear seems all too real. However, once we step out of the theatre, we realize that the heroes and heroines are nowhere to be seen. Despite this, we continue to discuss the movie until we return home and acknowledge that it was all just a fictional portrayal. It's a reminder of how we sometimes deceive ourselves in real life by not confronting the truth and convincing ourselves that everything is or will soon be fine.

It's akin to a pigeon pretending not to see a cat, assuming that if it can't see the cat, the cat can't see it. This illusion can prove to be fatal, just as the pigeon lost its life through this mistake. Understanding reality and stepping out of our fantasies is crucial for achieving success. Remaining stagnant and neglecting personal growth, expert guidance, and keeping a pulse on the competition is comparable to destroying the roots of our business instead of nurturing its growth. Embracing the present with transparency and authenticity is the hallmark of prosperous individuals. Failing to do so is akin to deceiving ourselves and will inevitably lead to dire consequences in the future. Procrastination is our real *enemy, preventing us from facing reality and leading to failure. While a strategy is like a blueprint, real facts are the foundation that turns our goals into reality. Without acknowledging and addressing real facts, achieving our goals is impossible.*

Mr. Dev, the vice president of the Electric Switch company, graciously invited us to the grand inauguration of his exquisite home. The event was attended by esteemed individuals from various fields. Upon entering Mr. Dev's home, it became apparent that every detail was meticulously crafted with dedication and care. From top - of-the-line luxurious floor marbles to the imposing chandeliers and lighting solutions, every aspect spoke of sophistication. The exclusive furniture and tasteful color combinations further enhanced the overall beauty of the house.

Mr. Dev's house is situated on a sloped piece of land, with three open sides and one side protected by a three-story dead wall. This wall shields the house from a mass of soil towering two stories high. Despite the considerable investment in constructing the dead wall, it lacks drainage holes. During the rainy season, water accumulation behind the wall could potentially pose a significant threat without proper drainage. I have informed Mr. Dev about *the necessity of having drain holes for the safety of the retaining wall. Despite suggestions from the construction experts, he has decided against incorporating them. Mr. Dev is concerned that the drain holes will allow mud to enter his open garden during rainy days. He believes that the high-grade concrete and additional steel used in construction will be sufficient to withstand water pressure, and he is confident that no damage will occur in the future. Upon revisiting my concern with Mr. Dev, he insisted that I join him for lunch.*

During the monsoon season, Mr. Dev contacted me about a significant crack in his wall and asked me to have a look urgently. Upon my arrival, I observed that the crack was substantial enough to pose a collapse risk to the three-story concrete wall. I advised Mr. Dev to keep himself and his family away from the wall due to its instability. Urging him to immediately engage a civil team to reinforce the wall, I emphasized the importance of commencing strengthening work without delay. Although Mr. Dev affirmed his commitment to my advice, the entire wall collapsed in the afternoon, causing damage to other parts of the house. Fortunately, no one was injured as they had all been at a safe distance. This incident underscored the consequences of ignoring crucial details and taking a lax approach. While it resulted in significant property damage, Mr. Dev gleaned a valuable lesson about the gravity of disregarding factual information and ignoring real facts.

Establishing timelines and setting limits is essential for achieving our goals sustainably and effectively. By implementing time limits, we can eliminate low-value activities that drain our time and energy. Avoiding these activities allows us to maintain a healthy work-life balance. Striking a balance between our professional and personal lives is crucial for our overall happiness and satisfaction. Setting limits helps us create a secure and efficient link between our efforts and our goal achievement. Limits play a pivotal role in the execution of our strategy, enabling us to conserve energy, time, and effort. Just as adhering to speed limits on the road ensures a safe and relaxed journey, setting limits in our daily lives can guide us toward our goals in a controlled and sustainable manner.

The thermostat is essential for maintaining the optimal functioning of modern machinery. Without it, air conditioners would run continuously, leading to excessive cooling. When air conditioner compressors are overused, they can burn out and fail to provide cooling. Just as a small thermostat serves as a controller and shuts off machines to extend their lifespan and ensure safety, we must consider the impact on our bodies and minds of working continuously without a thermostat. It's evident that without proper breaks, our physical and mental well-being will suffer. To safeguard their longevity and functionality, we need to maintain our internal thermostat or timeline. Similar to how dams release excess water through floodgates to prevent structural damage, we must recognize our limits and boundaries of efforts. Just as a dam's integrity relies on managing water levels, our well-being depends on setting and respecting personal limits. Without acknowledging and adhering to these limitations, we risk overwhelming ourselves, potentially leading to detrimental consequences.

Everything in life has its constraints, and it's essential to recognize and respect those boundaries to live a balanced and sustainable life. Setting limits and timelines is crucial for achieving our goals. These boundaries ensure that we allocate our time, resources, and energy efficiently, preventing us from becoming fixated on a single issue or solution. It's important to set limits in our food habits, such as controlling sugar, salt, carbohydrates, and protein intake to maintain good *health. Without a proper diet, we can feel weak, and excessive consumption can lead to weight gain and health issues. Setting limits is crucial in all aspects of life to understand our needs and avoid overindulgence. To achieve optimal fitness and become a successful bodybuilder, it's essential to dedicate time to various muscle groups like biceps, triceps, shoulders, chest, abs, back, and thighs. Focusing solely on one area can result in uneven muscle development. To attain the best results, it's necessary to limit the time spent on specific muscle groups and engage all of them for a balanced physique. Additionally, allowing adequate rest for muscle recovery is crucial.*

When embarking on the path to achieve our life goals, it is essential to set limits within each category of our planning. Dedicating time to different areas of focus each day instead of fixating on a single subject allows us to gain a comprehensive understanding of our overall plan or strategy. This approach enables us to identify any necessary adjustments or amendments early in the planning process. Successful individuals do not confine themselves to a single problem or subject. Instead, they allocate time and set time limits for each item on their agenda. If they find that a project or goal is not beneficial *for the future, they are not afraid to discard it and move on to the next challenge. Timelines and limits provide insight into the feasibility of plans in their initial stages, allowing us to progress to the next chapter of our lives without squandering valuable time.*

SOUL - OCEAN OF POSITIVITY

To truly connect with our soul's energy, it's essential to incorporate these 5 natural laws into our daily lives. Despite the challenges, criticisms, and setbacks we face, we must remain steadfast in upholding our core values. Just as slipping on a ladder can lead to an uncertain landing, allowing negativity into our lives can have unforeseen consequences. It's crucial to always reinforce these 5 natural laws to overcome stress and negativity. Just as a paper bag cannot hold a hundred gallons of water, and a wall made of butter cannot bear a hundred kgs of weight, we cannot embark on the right path without fortifying our character and conquering resentment, cupidity, and ego. Without reinforcing and practicing 5 natural laws, we are vulnerable to succumbing to the battles against stress and negativity.

By mastering the 5 natural laws, we can defeat the adversaries of stress and negativity, leading to the discovery of our radiant, wispy, pure soul filled with boundless positivity. Just as our soul is an ocean of positivity, continuously illuminating the right path for us, we must elevate our intellect to understand and absorb this positive energy. Without honing our skills and embracing these 5 natural law techniques, we are destined to be mistaken. It's like admitting a 10-year-old kid into college and without the necessary intellectual development, the 10-year-old kid cannot compete with college students. Similarly, we must develop the intellect to grasp higher levels of understanding.

To excel as a bodybuilder or athlete, consistent practice and a well-balanced diet are essential. However, simply consuming a balanced diet is not enough. Proper digestion and rest time routine are the keys to unlocking its benefits. Without efficient digestion, the energy needed for training and competition cannot be fully utilized. Similarly, without adequate rest for our bodies, minds, and muscles, no amount of daily diet or practice can prevent injuries or lead to winning medals. Exercise and practice, combined with a nutritious diet, are essential, but allowing our bodies and minds to rest is equally crucial for reaping the benefits of our efforts. we must ensure that we digest and process all the positivity within *us to lead fulfilling lives.*

Living a life of great success and abundance is something many of us aspire to achieve. However, it's important to acknowledge that reaching the top comes with great responsibilities and challenges. While the rewards are significant, maintaining our position and continuing to thrive requires unwavering commitment and resilience. It's crucial to align our values with our principles and work diligently to overcome our weaknesses. Even after reaching the peak, we must remain vigilant in protecting our positivity, as negative influences will always seek to undermine our success. By staying focused on positivity and fortifying our inner strength, we can ensure our continued triumph in life.

One of our housemaid daughters flew to the US for advanced studies in business management. Before her departure to the US to pursue advanced studies in business management, the daughter of our housemaid joined us for dinner. During our meal, I asked her how she managed to achieve so much given her family's educational and financial limitations. She smiled at my direct question and proceeded to share her secret to success.

She shared that she always had a big dream in her

heart to study abroad, but due to her family's financial issues, she never shared her dreams with anyone. She faced many struggles in her life, losing her father at a young age and then watching her mother become the sole breadwinner for the family. As the eldest of her two younger brothers, the financial crisis was a constant presence since her childhood. She revealed that at times, she would only eat a small portion of food at night to ensure her younger brothers and mother had enough to eat. Through these experiences, she learned the truth of life that food tastes best when you are hungry, and for her, every meal, no matter how it was prepared, was satisfying because it filled her hunger. She observed many wealthy people leaving food on their plates, claiming it wasn't tasty, but for her, every morsel was valuable because it alleviated her hunger.

To support her mother financially, she began working alongside her to clean homes. Their hard work led to taking on more houses. Despite the long hours and late nights spent completing school work, her determination to excel and study abroad at a top university never wavered. Her unwavering drive to succeed, both academically and professionally, motivated her to save from her earnings and cover her school expenses. Achieving top grades in school, passing government exams, and working tirelessly, she continued to pursue her dream of studying business at a prestigious university. Her dedication paid off when she received a scholarship to a top university in the US.

Her dedication, focus, and hunger for success deeply inspired me and my family. We wish her the best in her future endeavors. She taught me that hunger is essential for success in life. Without hunger, we cannot recognize our emptiness or the need for something in our lives. Our efforts multiply when there is a strong desire, enabling us to solve everyday problems and find solutions. Her hunger to study abroad kept her resilient, even on an empty stomach, she never slept without completing her schoolwork. Her drive persisted even when she was earning more than others around her. Her perseverance was rewarded when she gained admission to her dream university.

INTELLECT – A FRIEND

As the rulers of planet Earth, humans possess an extraordinary gift bestowed upon us by the supreme power is - our intellect. This unique trait sets us apart from all other species, allowing us to dominate our planet.

However, our journey does not end here. We are now seeking to expand our dominion to other planets. Yet, amidst our quest for interplanetary exploration, we find ourselves entangled in internal conflicts, struggling for survival. The very intellect that elevated us above all other species is now driving us to compete amongst ourselves. After subduing every other species on Earth, we are now locked in a battle for supremacy within our ranks. It's incorrect to blame our intellect for the chaos within ourselves. Our intellect has propelled us to the top of the species, enabling us to achieve remarkable milestones and survive the toughest situations. Competition is inherent to our nature, but we must harness our positive energy and intellect to pursue what is right. If we misuse our positive energy and intellect, the outcome will always be negative. By combining positive energy and intellect for the right cause, we can achieve ultimate success. We've already learned 5 natural laws to promote positivity and overcome stress and negativity. Now, choosing the right cause is the final step or hurdle before making our life grand and successful.

After mastering various strategies for thriving in the face of challenges and embracing positivity, the final step towards reaching the pinnacle of inner peace is to engage our intellect through thoughtful reflection. Our journey has encompassed honing coping mechanisms, resisting negativity, recognizing positive cues, maintaining life balance, and pursuing our life's objectives. It's important to recognize that individuals with a strong intellect will seek to understand and rationalize before fully embracing concepts or principles. Meanwhile, those with a more straightforward approach may readily accept and adhere to rules and laws. Thus, people blessed with intellectual acumen must feed their intellect through exposure to diverse opportunities, experimentation, and resources to facilitate their personal growth. Failing to nourish their intellect could impede their inner journey, acting as a barrier or even an adversary.

By satisfying the intellect, it can transform into an invaluable ally, propelling us forward at an accelerated pace. Regardless of whether our intellect is straightforward or profound, ensuring its contentment paves the way for an easier journey. When questions or uncertainties cloud our minds regarding principles or laws, we must address them through thorough reasoning to dispel any doubts. While individuals with a simple intellect may be easily swayed by external influences, those with a fortified intellect steadfastly stand by their decisions. Thus, satisfying our intellect is paramount to fostering unwavering resolve and hope.

By delving deep into knowledge, nurturing positive thoughts, and embracing real facts with unwavering faith, we can begin to satisfy our intellect. True fulfillment comes from embracing the power of positivity, walking the path with honesty, and experiencing the transformative effects on our environment and outcomes. Adhering to the 5 natural laws will bring ultimate satisfaction and strengthen our faith and hope. In order to stay true to our practice, we must avoid allowing our intellect to be unsatisfied, which can lead us astray and make us susceptible to distractions. Committing to the 5 natural laws and remaining faithful to them will lead us to achieving our life goals and securing a better future.

Our decisions shape our destiny. It is our responsibility to choose our path, determine our aspirations, and take action. Our soul provides us with the positive energy and strength to pursue our goals. The outcomes we achieve are a reflection of the objectives we set. Our soul transcends human emotions and is a force that guides us beyond transient feelings of happiness, sorrow, or success. It is imperative to carefully select our goals and adhere to the 5 natural laws that govern our well-being.

Making sound choices is vital, as it directly impacts not only our fulfillment but also the lives of those we cherish.

To conquer the final obstacles and discover our true purpose, we must attune ourselves to our inner voice and emotions. Our soul speaks a language of love, devoid of hate for any being. As children, we loved everyone around us unconditionally, and this love is the essence of our soul. Embracing and sharing love allows it to thrive and grow within us. Our soul communicates with us through our feelings. It is a wellspring of boundless love, ever-increasing, never diminishing, and spreading endless positivity and compassion.

We all adore children, but can we truly comprehend a mother's love and deep connection with her child? This extraordinary bond and profound emotion can only be experienced and understood by the mother and her child. It emanates directly from the soul, an invaluable sentiment that cannot be bought or sold. When we extend a helping hand to those in need, how does it make us feel? Can we effectively convey these emotions to others or express them within our social circles? The truth is, we can never fully articulate these profound sentiments. It is only the giver who can truly experience the love and fulfillment that comes from within. Similarly, when we set a path or goal for ourselves, we are surrounded by options. Our soul will send us blissful and bright signals if the goal is right, No one other than us can experience those feelings or emotions of peace. Always remember, it is as easy to choose the right goal as it is to choose the wrong one. However, the result of the wrong goal or aim will always be unsatisfactory, while the outcome of walking the path to achieve the right goal will always be bright and satisfactory.

WISE USE OF POSITIVE POWER

In our modern world, the uses of energy are indispensable. We rely on electricity, fossil fuels, and natural gas for almost every aspect of our daily lives. These vital resources are sourced from diverse outlets and undergo various production methods before they are harnessed to enhance human comfort. By employing energy in agricultural machinery, we can yield an abundance of food. Utilizing energy in our household gadgets and tools can enhance our quality of life while fuelling vehicles enables us to cover great distances and connect with our loved ones. If we use energy wisely to power our machines, gadgets, and tools, we can unlock countless benefits. However, if we channel this power into bombs and bullets, it can have devastating consequences, taking lives and causing destruction. The way we use energy determines its impact. When we utilize our positive energy for good and noble purposes, the results are always positive. Conversely, directing positive energy toward dark desires, harming others, or unethical actions will always yield negative outcomes.

When we channel our positivity into negative activities, the result will always be negative. It's crucial to direct our positive energy in the right direction and avoid squandering it on the wrong tasks. To achieve this, we must strive to calm our energetic minds and avoid misusing our positive energy. Daily meditation can help us achieve the necessary relaxation and focus. By closing our eyes and turning our attention inward, we can free our minds from external distractions and attachments. This simple practice will help us center our thoughts and find the right path.

As we navigate the responsibilities and decisions that come with mastering the 5 natural laws and developing a strong character, we must remain vigilant against the potential for our past experiences and habits to influence our decision-making process. While reaching top positions brings a new level of responsibility, it also requires us to transition from receiving orders to giving them. It's crucial to recognize that our past habits and tendencies can resurface when we are in a top or strong position to make decisions, potentially impacting the outcomes in ways that may not align with our goals. To minimize the impact of our past experiences on our decision-making, we must carefully evaluate our actions before issuing directives to others. This self-examination is crucial in ensuring that our decisions are based on positivity and serve the best interests of all involved.

One of my good friends, Mr. Kale, paid me an unexpected visit at my office. This was unusual as we usually met during our free time or while exercising or doing yoga. However, I was more than happy to take a break from work to catch up with him. Mr. Kale is a retired individual who used to work for the dam management board. Despite his age, he was incredibly fit and possessed impressive stamina, surpassing even the younger individuals during our exercise and yoga sessions. Upon entering my office, I noticed that Mr. Kale seemed quite tense. He confided in me about his son's financial troubles and sought my advice. I immediately reassured him and offered him a glass of water to calm his nerves. It turns out that his son had suffered significant financial losses in the cryptocurrency market, which led him to quit his job and return home. Mr. Kale was deeply concerned about his son's well-being, suspecting that deeply disturbed by financial losses he may be suffering from depression, and struggling to find a way out of his current situation. Mr. Kale requested that I accompany him to his house and speak with his son, seeking my guidance and support during this challenging time.

When we arrived at Mr. Kale's house, I found his son sitting in a dimly lit room, engrossed in something on his laptop. Mr. Kale and I entered his son's room, and I noticed that he was still focused on crypto stocks on his laptop. I inquired with Mr. Kale's son about the cause of and reasons behind the losses. Mr. Kale's son explained that in the first few months, he observed small fluctuations in crypto stocks and decided to invest some of his money. After a year, he witnessed a significant surge in crypto stocks, with his investment increasing tenfold. Excited by this tremendous gain, he proceeded to invest all his money with the expectation of multiplying his wealth overnight. Initially, the crypto stocks continued to rise, but after a week, they took a sharp downturn, plummeting to their lowest levels.

This downward trend persisted for a week, and instead of responding to the steep decline, he clung to the hope of recovering his hard-earned money, which eventually evaporated in the market. Subsequently, in shock, he quit his job and returned home. His story was disheartening, and as a noob to the crypto market, he lost all his savings. I advised him that relinquishing his job and fixating on the crypto market would not yield any gains. I urged him to promptly seek new employment, if possible. Additionally, I suggested that he focus on employing the 5 natural laws to combat his stress and negativity. He was acutely aware of the immense stress he was under and sought guidance on coping strategies. Consequently, he promptly accepted my offer. I also made him promise to refrain from pursuing stocks for at least the next six months. I urged him to distance himself entirely from the market and concentrate on his areas of expertise.

I asked him to do that because, during a professional meeting last year, I met Mr. Gautam, the head of the Sales and Marketing division at a power tool company. He explained that until last year, their sales figures were plummeting and the company's profits were in very bad shape. Upon closer examination, they discovered that some products weren't selling at all, while others were *facing stock availability issues. In both cases, the company couldn't generate sales figures even though the market was booming and competitors were performing well in all segments. After reviewing the report, Mr. Gautam made a decisive move to stop ordering stock of inventory items that were not selling well and instructed the sales team to focus on products with stock availability issues. He advised the board of directors to double the stock of products facing availability issues compared to last year and to avoid selling the dead inventory for the first half of the year. The board accepted his decision, and thanks to the backhand team's complete focus on those products and improved stock availability, sales figures turned around from red to black. After six months of significant growth in sales and positive profit figures, Mr. Gautam proposed selling the dead inventory at heavily discounted rates and recommended discontinuing those product lines. Mr. Gautam's proposal was accepted by higher management, leading to a directive for the sales force to sell and earn incentives on dead inventory material. Heavy discounts enticed customers to purchase more material than needed, while the sales team actively promoted the dead inventory to earn incentives. Mr. Gautam's decision to focus on winning products and cease focusing on dead inventory resulted in significant profits for the organization.*

I learned a valuable lesson from Mr. Gautam's experience. By focusing on profitable products and avoiding dead inventory, his company was able to achieve significant profits. Similarly, if we set aside our losses, bad habits, and poor decisions, and concentrate on building our strengths by embracing good habits and making the right decisions, we can become stronger and more capable of addressing our challenges. Only when we are in a position of strength should we tackle our weaknesses. Trying to handle both the good and the bad simultaneously is never a wise or effective approach to life. Additionally, Mr. Kale's son distanced himself from the crypto market, practiced the 5 laws, and focused on his strengths and positivity. In just four months, he received a job offer and rejoined the workforce. He expressed to his father that while the crypto market may be lucrative, he will keep his distance until he learns from professionals, choosing instead to focus on his career.

People who have had more positive experiences tend to approach life with a calmer and more positive outlook. On the other hand, those with more negative experiences may view the world through a negative lens, taking longer to make decisions and often feeling limited in their options. Embracing more positive experiences can lead to greater opportunities and a willingness to take risks while dwelling on negative experiences can hold us back. A positive mindset can open doors and lead to a brighter future. It's amazing how unforgettable moments with our families can be, like stepping in to help and driving everyone to dinner, shopping, or a movie. These spontaneous outings become cherished memories that stay with us for a lifetime. Life is full of both good and bad experiences, but it's the ones that leave a lasting impression that shapes our actions and decisions. Creating a positive environment has a significant impact on our mindset and actions. In positive surroundings, people are more inclined to take risks and flourish. On the contrary, a negative environment can lead to fear of failure and reluctance to try new things. It's essential to seek advice and improvement ideas from everyone around us, regardless of their position or background. While we should consider all ideas, the power of decision always remains with us. Embracing a continuous learning mindset and expanding our skill set can lead us to achieve remarkable success and become a source of inspiration for others.

RIGHT DECISION AT RIGHT TIME

Full of positivity and possessing a strong character, it's important to avoid overconfidence. Some individuals have mastered the 5 natural laws and fallen into the trap of overconfidence. While they have achieved significant success in their careers, finances, relationships, and social circles, viewing oneself as an expert can hinder further growth. Considering oneself an expert can lead to taking others and their advice for granted. This can cause missed opportunities for improvement and progress. Although our decisions may yield positive results and minimize mistakes, reaching our goals can take various paths. Choosing the fastest route can save time, energy, and effort that can be used for other tasks such as leisure, family time, or self-improvement.

When we embrace positive energy, we naturally attract others to us. The transformation and growth of our character through the power of 5 natural laws draws people to us, expanding our social network. This journey of positivity leads us to connect with many friends and colleagues. A positive person inherently draws others towards them, especially in a society where many struggle with stress and negativity. People seek advice and guidance from positive individuals, leading to *meaningful discussions and exchanges of opinions. Helping to improve others' lives brings a deep sense of satisfaction and inner peace. However, when interacting with stressed and negative individuals, it's important to maintain our own beliefs and not let their perspectives influence us.*

In challenging environments, it's common to experience disruptions in our decision-making processes and value systems. While it's important to engage with others and offer guidance for improvement, it's equally vital to set limits on these interactions. Genuine change is reflected in modified behaviors and evolving discussions. As individuals embrace your positive suggestions, it's appropriate to engage in more profound conversations, signifying their acceptance and aspiration to follow a better path. On the contrary, if they remain steadfast in their ways, failing to progress despite your guidance, it's advisable to create some distance. Continuing to engage with such individuals only perpetuates a toxic cycle and may potentially cause uncertainty in our own beliefs.

We often witness the downfall of bright individuals who succumb to the influence of toxic people, leading to incarceration and ruined lives. Additionally, many otherwise grounded individuals have fallen victim to destructive habits like substance abuse and gambling due to negative social circles. These toxic individuals not only harm themselves but also spread their harmful influence, causing widespread damage to families and communities. It's crucial to recognize and avoid such negative influences to protect our well-being and the well-being of those around us.

By truly embracing the 5 natural laws, we can conquer our goals, achieve our dreams, and reach our targets while maintaining a balanced life. Each step of these laws is fueled by positive thoughts and character, propelling us towards success. Initially, as we achieve a series of successes, pride accompanies our journey through these unbeatable laws, we sometimes set unrealistic targets or have unrealistic expectations imposed upon us by family, friends, colleagues, and other influences in our lives. These unrealistic and superficial expectations lead us onto unknown horizons where the results often fall short of our desires.

It is entirely feasible to shift from a career in software engineering to pursuing full-time work in agriculture, but such a transition will necessitate a gradual and thorough approach, along with mental and physical preparation. Adjusting to the demands of an agricultural environment, which includes enduring direct sunlight, rain, and harsh weather, is a substantial departure from the controlled setting of a software engineer's workspace. Maintaining motivation in the face of these new challenges is certainly a considerable task, particularly for individuals accustomed to a pristine, dust-free work environment and moderate temperatures, not to mention the freedom to enjoy coffee at any time. Alternatively, taking on a role overseeing a team of software professionals or launching your software enterprise may present a more pragmatic approach. This path would allow for the utilization of your well-honed skill set and positive energy. If we're involved in agriculture or have relevant experience, it's important to focus our positive energy on growing our agriculture business. We've seen individuals from diverse industries successfully transition and thrive. While ambitious goals are achievable, it's crucial to consider our skill set, strengths, weaknesses, past experiences, team dynamics, and market conditions before solidifying our life goals or targets.

GREAT FEAT AND NEVER COLLAPSE

FEAT stands for Focus Effort Action and Technique. With our focused efforts to understand the 5 laws that help us combat the challenges of this new era, it's time to put in 100% honest efforts to practice them and make them an integral part of our lives. Our consistent efforts will deepen our understanding of negativity and its impact. Through proper action and implementation of these 5 laws, we will learn how to conquer our daily battles. Using techniques to overpower stress and negativity, we will experience a different world perspective. Positivity will surround us, and everyone will act as a positive force to help us naturally achieve our life goals.

Now that we have learned, understood, and aligned our goals with the 5 natural laws, it's time to take consistent action every day to transform our lives with positive energy. Just like conquering Everest takes time, we must commit to honest daily efforts to align ourselves with the powerful force driving the universe. A great achievement awaits us, and we must harness the stream of positivity to succeed. Let's not block the flow of positive energy. Instead, let's use it to our advantage, just like riding the current of a river. Utilizing the current of positive energy will bring abundance and actualize the life we've always dreamt of.

Incorporating leisure, independence, and breathing space into our lives is necessary for our well-being.

Embracing the 5 laws doesn't mean neglecting family time, social gatherings, or letting go of our routines. It's about finding harmony in all aspects of life. Just as living by the 5 laws is important, taking breaks is equally crucial. These breaks not only rejuvenate us but also bring creativity and new energy into our lives. Whether it's taking a day off or going on a week-long trip with friends, these experiences enrich our lives without compromising our values. Routine can lead to monotony, so it's vital to carve out time for ourselves. By allowing ourselves these breaks, we can appreciate the beauty and joy of life. Embracing the 5 laws and prioritizing leisure activities can help us lead fulfilling lives and maintain a positive mindset. Trying new experiences and taking calculated risks can add vibrancy and spontaneity to our lives. Living our lives according to the 5 laws not only brings positivity into our own lives but also positively influences our family environment. When we embody these laws, our children are more likely to follow our lead and readily agree to our suggestions aimed at improving their lives. While challenges and struggles are inevitable, they cannot break us if we maintain our self-belief and uphold our strong values.

It is crucial to make thoughtful and well-informed

decisions. Acting sensibly, without haste, and with a deep understanding of the facts is essential. By embracing and mastering these 5 natural laws, we can unlock extraordinary personal and professional growth. These laws are inherent to us, much like our shadows are inseparable from our bodies. Embracing these natural laws and harmonizing with them in pursuit of our life goals becomes effortless when we embark on a journey from darkness to light with an internal perspective. Cultivating a positive mindset and heeding the ever-present whispers of positivity within us enables us to soar to great heights, living life to the fullest according to the grand design of natural laws.

I remember a time when I was trekking in the Himalayas with a group of enthusiasts during the winter. We were facing intense cold and strong winds, feeling the fear of the harsh weather conditions. Our guide shared a valuable lesson with us about facing adversities. He emphasized that although we couldn't change the cold, we could keep ourselves warm by continuously walking and maintaining a clear focus on overcoming the challenges. He inspired us to persist in our journey back to our tents and made us realize that no adverse weather could harm us if we maintained our positive mindset and determination to reach our destination. That day, I learned that when problems seem insurmountable, even a tiny step toward our goal brings us one step closer to victory.

We should all adopt a never-collapse attitude, no matter how difficult the situation or problem may seem. Taking one step at a time towards finding a solution is crucial. A defeatist mindset is extremely harmful. Despite having the capabilities to overcome life's challenges, many of us succumb to negative thoughts, believing that we can't succeed. A negative attitude or a defeatist mindset is not constructive. A resilient and never-give-up attitude empowers us to take action and achieve great heights in life.

Q & A

<u>*Q. Can you say something about stress and negativity in brief?*</u>

The root of stress and negativity lies within our own thoughts. Unlike diseases acquired from external sources such as food, air, or water, stress and negativity stem from our internal mindset. By making changes to our environment, diet, and hygiene, we can address external issues. However, to tackle stress and negativity, we must adopt an inside-out approach, focusing on cultivating positive and resilient thoughts within ourselves. This shift will enable us to perceive the world in a more optimistic light, ultimately alleviating our internal struggles.

<u>*Q. I have been under considerable stress for quite some time, and despite my efforts to overcome it, it seems to persist no matter what I do. It feels as though my stress*</u>

and negativity has become deeply rooted within me, and I am struggling to overcome them.

It's essential to recognize that stress and negativity are not real or physical issues, but rather illusions we create in our perception of reality. A positive individual can learn to drive a car quicker than a negative person who harbors fear. Both are equally capable of driving, but the difference lies in their thought patterns: one seeks positivity and is unafraid of taking risks, while the other embraces negativity and succumbs to fear.

Taking small steps and being patient with yourself can make a big difference. You have the strength to overcome this, even when it seems challenging. I completely understand how you feel. It's not easy to deal with stress and negativity, especially when it feels like it's been lingering for a long time. However, it's important to remember that Buried deep within us is an ocean of positivity, and stress and negativity merely act as a superficial cover over the light within us. Uncovering this light allows us to feel and see the positivity inside.

There are strategies and techniques that can help you overcome these feelings, and it's possible to find relief. I encourage you to explore 5 laws and incorporate them into your life - doing so will bring about a noticeable *change in your surroundings and overall environment.*

<u>*Q. Why do we need to abide by 5 natural laws when positivity can conquer all negativity?*</u>

The power of positivity can significantly impact personal growth and contribute to a happier world. It's important to distinguish between bringing positivity into our lives and embodying a positive mindset. While embracing positivity might come naturally to some, maintaining that positive outlook requires practice and skill. Understanding and applying the five natural laws can fortify our resilience against negativity and its influence on our lives. By adhering to these laws, we can pave the way for a more positive and fulfilling existence.

Your book states that all successful people have followed the same rules to achieve success in their lives, could you explain that?

Just as there are different routes to reach Paris, there are countless paths to achieving our life goals and aspirations. Each individual possesses a unique combination of strengths and weaknesses, and it's essential to find the most effective approach to unlock our *potential for success and fortunes.*

Q. How can we better accept situations in our lives through 5 natural laws?

Well, that is what 5 natural laws are training us to do, 5 laws are nothing but training our mind to keep balance in our life during situations of joy and misery. 5 laws help us in not get lost in the world of pleasure and pain. We worry about things that we do not want to happen in our lives. With the understanding of 5 natural laws and with practice, we can chalk out our future routes. We all have certain desires, certain wishes, certain ambitions, and certain goals to achieve in life. The purpose of 5 natural laws is to train our mind, body, and soul to adopt that attitude of accepting, living, maintaining, and developing a vibe of positivity in our life.

Q. Could you elaborate on bad choices and bad company?

Making poor decisions is something that can happen to anyone at any stage of their life. These choices can stem from feelings of resentment, greed, and ego, and can have a detrimental impact on one's livelihood if not addressed. Even wise individuals can fall victim to these negative influences, leading to a significant decline in their once prosperous and harmonious lives. Such decisions often bring about pessimism and suffering.

Furthermore, associating with the wrong crowd is a consequence of poor decision-making. It is imperative to distance oneself from such influences as soon as possible. By removing ourselves from negative environments and embracing a positive way of life, we can eventually serve as a guiding light for others. Only by ensuring our own well-being first can we effectively help and inspire others to pursue the right path. These decisions and associations can lead to a misalignment of values and a breakdown of trust in our lives.

Q. What is the best attitude to learn and practice 5 natural laws?

Initial faith serves as the foundation for all endeavors. As we enter the educational system, we place our trust in our teachers and in the belief that achieving high grades will lead to a better life. However, genuine faith is only realized when we become self-sufficient breadwinners. By embracing honesty, commitment, and dedication to mastering the 5 natural laws, we discover true internal satisfaction and can develop unwavering faith in these principles, ultimately unlocking the essence of life.

Q. It seems there are too many facets in understanding the positivity of life, could you explain this?

Embracing the multitude of choices in life often leads us astray from the right path. By aligning ourselves with the guiding principles of the 5 natural laws, we can nurture our souls with boundless positivity. Positivity, with its divine and unique essence, holds the key to unlocking our inner strength, empowering us to overcome life's trials and tribulations. It has the remarkable ability to enrich our lives with love, joy, and happiness. Upon experiencing its transformative impact, we come to realize that we alone hold the power to truly understand and embrace positivity.

Q. Is it advisable to practice other rules and laws suggested and written by global experts?

Investing time in honing your skills and broadening your understanding is always advantageous. However, it is crucial to be mindful of the impact of our thoughts, as they can potentially lead us astray. Merely going through the motions without genuine dedication and commitment will not lead to significant change unless we wholeheartedly embrace these principles. Our personal experiences will inherently reflect our level of commitment and honesty in practicing these principles. We should spend as much time possible to satisfy our thoughts, but once we have taken it upon ourselves to follow them, then we must give it a fair trial.

Q. Can you tell us the function of 5 natural laws?

Like a train engine that takes all coaches at the same speed, without discrimination, the five natural laws propel our internal journey to discover our ultimate source of positivity—the soul. When we connect with this ocean of positivity, achieving our desires, life goals, and aims becomes attainable while maintaining balance in our lives. It's essential to embrace this positivity within us to lead a fulfilling and purposeful life.

Q. What do you mean by Soul the "Ocean of Positivity"?

It is a metaphor for the interconnectedness of our life in our world. The vastness of the world's oceans mirrors the profound impact they have on sustaining life. Oceans play a critical role in shaping weather patterns, providing essential rainfall that nourishes the land and provides us with drinking water, and supporting the growth of food on land. Life itself is intricately linked to the oceans, as they serve as a fundamental component for sustaining life, the existence of life, from the smallest organisms to humans, relies heavily on the oceans. It's plausible that the absence of oceans on other planets contributes to the absence of discovered life forms beyond our own planet.

All progress in the world, and how we have evolved since ancient times or the inception of time, is commendable and is a result of positivity. Without positivity, there would be no faith and hope in life, which ultimately results in no progress for humankind. Our souls are akin to a compass needle, consistently pointing towards positivity. Just as a magnet is drawn to the north, our souls are instinctively inclined towards positivity. This natural alignment reflects a universal language perpetuating a collective drive for positivity.

Q. What will happen if we cannot find our ocean of positivity even after practicing 5 natural laws?

If we are unable to discover our ocean of positivity even after following the five natural laws, it may indicate that we need to reassess our approach. It could mean that there are other factors at play that need to be addressed in order to fully embrace positivity. It might be helpful to seek guidance from others, reevaluate our mindset, and explore new strategies for cultivating positivity. Remember that finding our ocean of positivity is a journey, and sometimes it takes time and effort to reach that destination.

Life unfolds in diverse ways, and success can manifest in various forms and at different paces. This does not diminish our accomplishments. No individual experiences only misery without a single moment of joy. Circumstances may vary, and some may encounter more obstacles while others lead more comfortable lives. For instance, in a classroom where all students study the same subjects under the same teacher, each student's academic performance differs. Although the learning materials and teaching methods remain consistent, each student's grasp of the material varies. Some grasp concepts swiftly, while others require more time. With persistent effort, every individual will progress steadily towards their goals.

Q. I find that it is very easy to get enthusiastic about 5 natural laws initially but it is difficult to sustain the enthusiasm.

Well, that is perfectly right. These 5 natural laws are so simple and convincing that we find that they are for us.

Our lives are full of ups and downs, and we get influenced by our partners, our social circles, our relations, and our surroundings. We should not be influenced by anybody to run to the path. It is an individual fight against stress and negativity, and we must find our strength from within. We must satisfy our thoughts from every aspect. Unless our thoughts are satisfied, they will come our way and it will be difficult to keep our enthusiasm.

If we are easily influenced by one another, then we find the enthusiasm very hard to keep. We should never be hasty. Satisfaction with the thoughts will give us faith and hope, and faith and hope will automatically guide us toward practice.

Q. What is your favorite technique or highly recommended approach to hit 100% success by practicing 5 natural laws?
I think the key to achieving 100% success by practicing the 5 natural laws is to truly understand and believe in these laws. It's also important to consistently and punctually apply these laws in your life. All the techniques are equally important, and by having faith in the natural laws and staying regular in your efforts, you can increase your chances of success significantly.